THE ALPHASCAN 2000

A New Approach to Numerology

SALVATORE STALLONE

D0839763

TAYLOR PUBLISHING COMPANY
DALLAS, TEXAS

Library of Congress Cataloging in Publication Data Stallone,
Salvatore.
    The Alphascan 2000.
    1. Symbolism of numbers. I. Title. II. Title: Alphascan two
thousand.
BF1623.P9S75   1985   133.3'35   85-4650
ISBN 0-87833-471-8 (soft)

Printed in the United States of America

FIRST EDITION   9 8 7 6 5 4 3 2 1

ACKNOWLEDGEMENTS

The author wishes to express his gratitude to all the individuals who have contributed to this effort and offered support during the creation of this presentation of *The Alphascan 2000*. For the part each of them has played, I wish to thank Sherry Hoenig, Debbie Housholder, Robert L. Miller, the editors and staff at Taylor Publishing Company, and to my family and friends who put up with me through it all.

CONTENTS

THE
ALPHASCAN
2000

INTRODUCTION

THE LEGACY OF PYTHAGORAS

Mathematicians and scientists who have investigated the contributions of the early mathematician/philosopher Pythagoras to our understanding of number theory have traditionally found it difficult to deal with his more esoteric applications of number logic. While principles such as the Pythagorean Theorem, which explains the relationship of the sides of a right triangle, have become fundamental to the study of modern geometry, theories of Pythagoras which approach deeper, more metaphysical levels have never been fully understood.

The truth is, number logic is doubtlessly the most fundamental of all sciences. An understanding of the importance of numbers underlies every calculation we make, from telling time and buying a cup of coffee to extrapolating the orbit of satellites. Numbers and their values influence our very thought and action in one way or another, and beyond mere mathematics, numbers have power to shape and explain the events of our daily lives.

That is essentially what Pythagoras discovered some 2,500 years ago. The fact that most of us have never learned to apply "number science" in the forms developed by Pythagoras and his predecessors does not diminish the value of his discoveries nor limit the influence of numbers upon us. However, the fact that contemporary society has been largely unable to call upon the instructive qualities of number science to assess and perceive ourselves and our environment, due to lack of exposure, ignorance and even prejudice, has no doubt limited our enjoyment of the world around us.

The basic principles of number science existed before Pythagoras and have continued long after him, although he was certainly one of the most eloquent practitioners of the science. For a period of time, from the eighteenth century on, numerology became an intriguing curiosity in some circles, a parlor game much like the Ouija board, but little more. At the same time, fortune tellers experimented with the predictive qualities of numbers without a deeper understanding of the panorama of applications of numbers in our lives and, by confusing and corrupting the science, gave numerology a bad name which it bears to this day.

The Alphascan 2000 is not born of any cult, intrigue or idle curiosity but of a natural fascination with the undeniable influences and interactions of numbers upon us. While this presentation owes a great debt to the legacy of those early philosophers, and while a genuine appreciation for the possibilities of number science almost demands a study of those first precursors, the Alphascan 2000 is a new and direct approach which will enable anyone with the capacity to judge impartially and without prejudgment to gain greater insight into themselves, their peers, and the world round them.

The Alphascan 2000 is metaphysical in the sense that it is an investigation of the nature of being as it is perceived by abstract reasoning. It is not *per se* a philosophy, in that it posits no fundamental set of values or perceptions of the essential nature or purpose of mankind, but its principles can be applied philosophically for self-betterment and for a deeper and fuller enjoyment of life.

The qualities and logical applications of numbers are eternal values which have existed since the beginnings of time. The God who created our world, in all its order and balance, created the foundations of all our sciences and gave us the ability to measure and explain our world through language, through intuition, and through the logic of numbers. Just as we are limited in our finite understanding of the absolute nature of things, we may not understand why numbers work the way they do or how the Creator imbued them with such marvelous powers of clarification and prediction, but they do work.

For many of you the Alphascan 2000 may remain a sort of game, and that is certainly agreeable to the author; but others may find here a certain sense of order and balance which helps to explain many things in your life which would otherwise be mysterious and unclear. That is perhaps the most rewarding application of this treatise and one which I hope will provide you with years of enjoyment and satisfaction. The scope of this work is designed to provide a complete perspective on self-expression, your goals and ambitions, your immediate and future environment, your friends and associates, and a general view of the possibilities which lie ahead. The charts and worksheet provided in the text allow each reader to create a visual analysis of each of these various categories, a graphic representation which can be referred to periodically and up-dated for specific purposes and events.

In the long run, this work is a practical system developed through serious, critical study and thought, and attempts to render some justice to the mathematical systems that modern science has forgotten. If this book enables each reader to gain some greater insight into the mysteries of his or her own life, and allows each one to gain an expanded appreciation for the logical tools we carry with us each day, it will have served its purpose.

THE MYSTICAL LINK

The Alphascan 2000 is the study of the meanings of numbers. It is often used to uncover secret events or to forecast the future. When so used, the Alphascan 2000 is a form of for-tune telling. Some of the elements of number science may be found in such practices as astrology, cartomancy (the use of playing cards), geomancy (use of figures or lines), and dream interpretation, when dream symbols are reduced to numbers. The common element in each of these is number logic and the interpretation of number values.

The Pythagorean system proposed that everything in our universe is based on numbers. Modern science has penetrated the secrets of sub-atomic particles and the ways in which mass and energy are inter-related in all forms of matter; yet, these qualities are always described in numerical terms. While there are fundamental differences between the use of quantitative and qualitative analysis through numbers, and between pure mathematical description and philosophical interpretation, the inter-relationships between the two are inevitable and were very much a part of the early Greek reasoning. For the Greeks, numbers were the mediator between the divine and the earthly; for us, they are the link between the intellectual and the physical.

To review the mystical link between number values and interpretations, consider the following. In American society, the number 13 is considered unlucky and all things somehow connected with 13 are to be avoided. The 13th day of the month, particularly if a Friday; the 13th Floor; 13 dinner guests; and so forth. A curious contrast occurs in Belgium where the number 13 is sometimes worn as a good luck charm.

The origin of the negative symbolism of 13 is often ascribed to the New Testament account of Judas as the 13th person at the Last Supper. But the number has a long history of mystical associations. It has been called the power and divinity number. It was considered a sacred number by some ancient societies and never mentioned indiscriminately. It was sometimes inscribed on amulets worn by mystics of the early Christian era and considered so holy that it came to be feared.

The 13 weeks of our four seasons mark the points of the square for building our calendar year. The great pyramid of Gizeh is built on 13 acres, has 13 tiers of stone at its entrance, its base measures 9,130 inches which, when the numbers are added together (or reduced), totals 13.

The United States is closely allied to the number 13. Its flag has 13 stripes to represent the 13 original colonies; its symbolic eagle has 13 arrows in one claw and a branch with 13 leaves in the other; 13 stars above its head and 13 stripes on its armor plate.

THE EARLY FOUNDATIONS OF NUMBERS

In the early Greek system, numbers from 1 to 10 had specific symbolic meanings as well as meanings in geometry, arithmetic, astronomy, acoustics, and thus in music. The term "music of the spheres" derives from the concept of mathematical relations among astronomical phenomena. Among the symbols represented by the number 1 were the first principle, the Creator, the East, unity, male-and-female, immortality, the right side, the day, the sun, and equality. The number 2 signified divisibility, female, the mortal, the left side, the night, the moon, inequality, and matter. Even numbers were characteristically female, odd numbers were male, an opposition reminiscent of the Chinese symbolism of Yang and Yin. The number 3, combining 1 and 2, represented perfection and stood for all reality, the unity of 1 and the diversity of 2.

In addition to the mystical meanings of numbers, another principle is basic to the Alphascan 2000: gematria, or cryptography. In Hebrew, consonants are used as numerical signs, but by providing them with vowels one can read numerical figures as words and, in turn, words as numbers. This allows readers of the Hebrew Bible to find hidden meanings in the text. Just such a combination of gematria and Pythagorean number symbolism was the basis of the number magic employed by the medieval Cabala.

Similar associations have been made with Greek and Latin figures, and to the Christian New Testament. Students of the Book of Revelations have explored the powerful attributes of the number 666, "the mark of the Beast." Curiously, this number also identifies such historical figures as Nero, Caesar, Pope Leo X, and Napoleon.

The Greek mathematicians' calculations established the theory of sound, the slant of the Zodiacal circle, our conception of the sun as the center of the universe and, in music, the diatonic scale. Their followers based their teachings on mathematics, music, and astronomy, which they considered to be the basis of all science and art. They also believed that mathematics could exist without music and astronomy, but that nothing could exist without numbers.

The systems used in contemporary number science have been around for several hundred years and have been augmented by European and American practitioners. The principle of "vibration," which relates sound to specific number values, holds that the meanings of numbers are related to the physical properties and musical qualities of utterance. Even though it is a complex phenomenon, the idea of vibration applies simply to the English alphabet and traditional number values. The numbers 1 through 9 are directly linked to the 26 letters of the alphabet and their interpretations have been adapted over centuries of experimentation and use. Quite simply, the system works.

THE ALPHASCAN 2000

The Alphascan 2000 is an art, or technique, of measurement. It is based on numbers as expressions of personality, goals, desires, actions, and the subconscious. The implications of these numbers, and manipulations of them, can be used to clarify talents, career choice, daily activities, and to predict the future. As a technique of measurement, the Alphascan 2000 can give you a plan of action and can act as a road map or guide to your special skills and abilities. Understanding the numbers in your life can encourage you when you feel frustrated or give you a green light when it's time to take action. The study of this simple technique will help you express your innate potential and make contributions to society which will return immeasurable rewards.

But before you begin your investigation of the Alphascan 2000, it is important that you understand what all the numbers stand for. The following review of number symbolism indicates the interpretations of the nine basic numbers. Further applications and manipulations using the Alphascan 2000 system will be added in subsequent chapters.

THE MEANINGS OF NUMBERS

The number 1 represents the beginning, a time for starting new things such as love, life, work and independence. When the number 1 appears in your chart it is a good time to shine;

this number is related to the sun. Constructively, the number 1 is ambitious, progressive and inventive. Negatively, the number 1 is egotistical, selfish and eccentric. Destructively, the number 1 is dominating, foolhardy and ruthless.

The number 2 is a combination of positive and negative forces. This is the emotional number, the number that forces a person to learn diplomacy and tact. When the number 2 appears in your chart it's time to wait and see, to let things come at their own speed. This number is associated with the moon. Constructively, the number 2 is understanding, receptive and cooperative. Negatively, the number 2 is vacillating, shy, self-effacing and over-sensitive. Destructively, the number 2 is deceitful, possessive and pessimistic.

The number 3 represents versatility. By combining the assets of numbers 1 and 2, the number 3 opens the door to progress. When number 3 appears in your chart, following through with projects is of the utmost importance. The number 3 is a green light allowing you to "go for it!" This number is associated with Jupiter. Constructively, the number 3 is artistic, sociable and enthusiastic. Negatively, the number 3 is critical, superficial and careless. Destructively, the number 3 is jealous, avaricious and deceitful.

The number 4 relates to the handling of details. When the number 4 appears in your chart it is time to slow down and concentrate on hard work. It is a number associated with routine, creative imagination and inner strength. Handled properly, this number has power. It is associated with Uranus. Constructively, the number 4 is determined, dependable and organized. Negatively, the number 4 is stubborn, self-righteous and phlegmatic (or apathetic). Destructively, the number 4 is dominating, ruthless and vulgar.

The number 5 represents change, communication and travel. When the number 5 appears in your chart it is time for creativity. It also expresses an attraction for the opposite sex, and the necessity of good ideas. Self-esteem is heightened with this number. This is a good number for climbing the ladder of life. The number 5 is associated with Mercury. Constructively, the number 5 is adaptable, progressive and resourceful.

Negatively, the number 5 is irresponsible, careless and thoughtless. Destructively, the number 5 is sensual, self-indulgent and malevolent.

The number 6 represents consummation and fulfillment. When the number 6 appears in your chart it is time to unite all forces, to protect the home, to be reunited with loved ones, and a time for the marriage of work, love, life and health. This is the number of diplomacy; a number which radiates the love of mankind. This number is associated with Venus. Constructively, the number 6 is sympathetic, just and conventional. Negatively, the number 6 is proud, worrysome and opinionated. Destructively, the number 6 is indulgent, malicious and jealous.

The number 7 is the number of self-deception, where life is sometimes accepted as it looks instead of how it really is. This is not a good number for partnerships, since it is dominated by illusion. The number 7 is a number of quantity not quality. It is associated with the planet Neptune. Constructively, the number 7 is intuitive, poised and spiritual. Negatively, the number 7 is critical, melancholy and skeptical. Destructively, the number 7 is deceitful, faithless and escapist.

The number 8 represents power. It pushes hard and puts stress on finances, achievement and business affairs. This is the best number for marriage; the rewards are as great as the effort one puts into it. The only way to lose with this number is to slow down. When the number 8 appears in your chart, do not think negatively; the key to power through this number is to think positively. It is a strong, all-encompassing number associated with Saturn. Constructively, the number 8 is an organizer, leader and balancer. Negatively, the number 8 is intolerant, ostentatious and strained. Destructively, the number 8 is unjust, unscrupulous and violent.

The number 9 may be either the beginning or the end. If one is very positive, then the number 9 represents completion and fulfillment; but if one thinks negatively, he or she may find a loss from what was learned in the lower numbers. When the number 9 appears in your chart it is a good time to finish all outstanding projects, but hold off on all new contracts until the cycle of 9 has passed. During the 9 cycle, avoid taking on other people's burdens and responsibilities, and throw out whatever you don't want. This is a time to think: you have a red light. This number is associated with Mars. Constructively, the number 9 is tolerant, humane and creative. Negatively, the number 9 is dissipating, over-emotional and egocentric. Destructively, the number 9 is morose, bitter and vulgar.

THE MASTER NUMBERS

When mathematically reduced, all numbers will add back to a single digit from 1 to 9. As an example, the sequence 123,456,789 when totalled adds up to 45 which reduces, in turn, to 9. All numbers, no matter how large or how small, can be reduced in this manner. There are two numbers, however, which have been discovered to have unique values that defy reduction: these numbers are 11 and 22. Because of their uniqueness and their special qualities, they have been designated as "Master Numbers." Even though each shares properties with their reduced values, 2 and 4, they have additional dimensions and generally should not be reduced.

The number 11 represents intuition. When this number appears in your chart you should go with your hunches. The number 11 also has strong influences for teaching others. This number encourages you to express your ideas, no matter how they sound, and to show your silver lining. This number is associated with Uranus. Constructively, the number 11 is intuitive, inspired and inventive. Negatively, the number 11 is aimless, impractical and cold. Destructively, the number 11 is fanatical, dishonest and degrading.

The number 22, the second master number, is the number of realization and actualization. When this number appears in your chart you have the full power to create for the attainment of life's master planes; to build your empire. During the 22 cycle you should avoid negative people. Even though this is a master number, beware! When everything is positive, the power of 22 is at its greatest strength. When it's a negative 22, the force of the 22 will turn to destroy everything around it.

This number is guided as if by astral war lords; it is associated with Pluto. Constructively, the number 22 is organizing, visionary and philosophical. Negatively, the number 22 is headstrong, dominating and material. Destructively, the number 22 is vengeful, criminal and vicious.

The peculiar qualities of numbers are often inexplicable and mystifying. Why they behave as they do and how they became associated with their unique properties is beyond our grasp. At the same time, there are mathematical oddities about these numbers which almost defy explanation. The number 9 is perhaps the strangest of all. If you multiply any number by 9 and total (or reduce) the answer to its lowest number, it will always return to 9. On the other hand, if you add, subtract, or divide the number 9 and reduce the answer you will always get the number you started with. The 9 seems almost to disappear into the cosmos. Examples: $12 + 9 = 21$, but 12 reduces to 3 and the total 21 also reduces to 3; $16 - 9 = 7$, but 16 reduces to 7; and 9 divided by 3 = 3. In each case, the 9 disappears.

When reducing numbers to their lowest value, something similar happens with 9: the 9 acts very much like a zero and disappears from the sum. As an example, total this sample of random numbers: 6 3 1 4 5 7 2. The total is 28 which reduces to 10 or 1. If we eliminate the numbers which total up to 9 (6+3, 4+5, 7+2), the only number left is 1, which is the reduced number we started with.

As a side note to this discussion of reductions with 9, it should be mentioned that this method of eliminating numbers which total to 9 can be a quick way to reduce numbers to their lowest value. However, for some of the computations which follow, the value of each number and letter will be important for analysis of complex symbols and messages and in these cases you should not eliminate or total-out numbers. Also, since 11 and 22 are master numbers, be careful of shortcuts which might reduce them to 2 or 4 without pausing to review their meanings as master numbers.

As a final comment on these mathematical oddities, it is interesting to note that all circles, the Earth, the Zodiac, and the rotation of the solar system, are based upon an orbit of 360 degrees: a number which reduces back to the mystical number 9. And once you discover the relationships beween our alphabet and the number values of individual letters, you will find that one of the most important words in the English language, LOVE, totals to 9.

Now that we have made at least a cursory review of the fundamentals of numbers and their historical meanings, we may begin our approach to the Mechanics of the Alphascan 2000 and ultimately to building your own Alphascan 2000 chart.

BUILDING
THE ALPHASCAN
2000

ALPHA 1

THE MECHANICS

All numbers are substantiated by symbols. They are also ruled by the planets. Number 1 is the Sun and Mars   ; 2 is the Moon   ; 3 is Venus and Mercury   ; 4 is Saturn   ; 5 is Mars   ; 6 is Jupiter   ; 7 is Neptune   ; 8 is Saturn   ; 9 is the Sun   ; 11 is Uranus   and the 22 is the planet Pluto

The Alphascan 2000 is the simple use of single digits and the numbers 10, 11, and 22, which have special meanings. The number 10 is considered the "bridge" between the first and second cycle of 9. It is the number that adds new impetus to what is termed, "the second spiral." Although its value is noted, it is reduced in practical use. The numbers 11 and 22 are "master numbers" and they are left unreduced in most positions in building the Alphascan 2000.

ALPHA 1 THE ALPHABETICAL KEY

A	B	C	D	E	F	G	H	I	1st, Degree
1	2	3	4	5	6	7	8	9	
J	K	L	M	N	O	P	Q	R	2nd, Degree
10	11	12	13	14	15	16	17	18	
S	·T	U	V	W	X	Y	Z		3rd, Degree
19	20	21	22	23	24	25	26		

A	B	C	D	E	F	G	H	I	1st, Degree
1	2	3	4	5	6	7	8	9	
J	K	L	M	N	O	P	Q	R	2nd, Degree
1	2	3	4	5	6	7	8	9	
S	T	U	V	W	X	Y	Z		3rd, Degree
1	2	3	4	5	6	7	8		

Using the alphabetical key in Alpha 1, we are now ready to find the various number values that can be derived from the full name. Although we are using an example name here, you will want to fill in your own name on the worksheets at the back of the book.

Before you start, it will be helpful to memorize the number value of each letter of the alphabet. Try to remember each number associated with each letter and practice saying them from top to bottom. Example: A = 1, J = 10, S = 19.

The first degree numbers are the first nine numbers and are the most uncomplicated in action.

A	B	C	D	E	F	G	H	I
1	2	3	4	5	6	7	8	9

The second degree numbers are the next nine numbers. These are the more involved ones.

J	K	L	M	N	O	P	Q	R
10	11	12	13	14	15	16	17	18

Third degree numbers are the last eight numbers. These are the most complicated and they are also more powerful.

S	T	U	V	W	X	Y	Z
19	20	21	22	23	24	25	26

VIBRATION

In learning the Alphascan, one must understand the principle of vibration which tells us that sound attracts quality and quantity and either harmony or discord. Your name vibrates constantly, as it is written, as it is thought, and as it is spoken. Everything we touch has a sound vibration. Even the earth has a distinctive vibration which increases at a rate of approximately one unit per week.

At the time you were born, you were given a name. Your name becomes a tool with which you meet life. The birth name indicates your abilities. If you change your name, or if someone has changed it for you, it can (and will) add or detract from your original birth name.

Each of us was born on a specific date. The date of birth shows our talents, what kind of vocation we will follow (or *should* follow) and what our life achievements and demands will be. In order to have a practical example to work from in developing this lesson, we will use a basic example name. How to arrive at these numbers will be explained further on in the lesson.*

ALPHA 2

THE NAME

Using the alphabetical key in Alpha 1, we are now ready to find the various number values that can be derived from the full name. Although we are using an example name here, you will want to fill in your own name on the worksheets at the back of the book.

$1+5+6+5 = 17 = 1+7 = 8$ $1+6+5 = 12 = 1+2 = 3$

	1		5	6	5			1		6	5	
S	A	L	V	E	T	O	R	E	(N)	S	T	A	L	L	O	N	E
1		3	4		2		9			5		1	2		3	3		5

$1+3+4+2+9 = 19 = 1+9 = 1$ 5 $1+2+3+3+5 = 14 = 1+4 = 5$

$113452695 = 9$ 5 $12133655 = 8$

The Desire — $8+3 = 11$

The Resource — $1+5+5 = 11$

The Expression — $9+5+8 = 22$

---

*I have changed the spelling of my first name for the example name so that it will have the greatest use for illustration purposes as we go along.

Before we proceed, let's learn one of the basic units of the Alphascan 2000, the vowels. The vowels include the letters A, E, I, O, U, plus, in certain instances, the letters Y and W. The letter Y is considered a vowel when it comes at the end of the name.

Example:

ay	by	cy	dy	ey	fy	gy	hy	iy
jy	ky	ly	my	ny	oy	py	qy	ry
sy	ty	uy	vy	wy	xy	yy	zy	

The letter Y may also be considered a vowel when it is the second letter of the name. Example: Lynn, Byron, Lynda, Myron, etc. But note: when the letter Y is the second letter of any name, you must assign it the value and function of the letter I; the number value becomes a 9 instead of its normal value of 7.

Example:

```
      I
      9
  L   Y   N   N          The letter I takes the
  3       5   5          place of Y.
```

The letter Y is also a vowel when it is at the beginning of a name and not followed by another vowel as in the name Yvette. The letter Y becomes a consonant when it is followed by another vowel, as in Yolanda.

The letter W may be a vowel as well, but only when it acts as a dipthong and follows another vowel.

Example: Ewing, Lawrence, Howard, etc.

The letter W as a Vowel: ew aw ow iw uw

Now that we have discussed the vowels, the next step is to review the consonants. The consonants are the rest of the alphabet without the vowels.

Example:

B	C	D	F	G	H	J	K	L
M	N	P	Q	R	S	T	V	(W)
X	(Y)	Z						

In calculating the various factors and values of the Alphascan, you will find that the vowels and consonants behave in distinctly different ways and provide very different messages about an individual's character and goals. In the following section, on the Desire, we will begin to see how these calculations will vary from section to section and person to person.

ALPHA 3

THE DESIRE

The Desire will give you an idea of what you desire in your life. Having the quality of the sun, like the power within yourself, the Desire is the force which allows you to aspire to whatever heights you wish to attain.

The Desire denotes your drive throughout life, your ambition and your goals. The Desire is what you wish to do, to be, and to know. Because the Desire is indicated by the vowels of your birth name, it reveals the life-giving and vitalizing part of your nature.

Let's start finding your Desire by using your name. First, write down your full name (first, middle, and last name). You will note that our example of SALVETORE N. STALLONE does not have a middle name, just an initial. Quite simply, the name is used in this form because it works best for the purposes of example without the middle name spelled out, just as the spelling of the first name has been changed for the example.

ALPHA 4

THE VOWELS

Example:

$1+5+6+5 = 17 = 1+7 = 8$ $\qquad\qquad 1+6+5 = 12 = 1+2 = 3$

A		E	O	E		A		0	E
1		5	6	5		1		6	5

S A L V E T O R E (N) S T A L L O N E

Note, the vowels are numbered at the top of the name.

The name SALVETORE N. STALLONE has vowels of A, E, O, and E for the first name. There are no vowels for the middle name. The last name has the vowels of A, E, and O. If your name has vowels in the middle name, be sure to put them down.

The first name has numbers that add up to 8. $1+5+6+5 = 17 = 1+7 = 8$. The middle name has no vowels, so we go on to the last name. The last name has numbers that add up to 3: $1+6+5 = 12 = 1+2 = 3$. Now that this step has been completed, we can add the total of the first name and the last name together.

Example: The first name adds up to 8, and the last name adds up to 3. Simply add the two together: $8+3 = 11$. The Desire for SALVETORE N. STALLONE is 11.

ALPHA 5

11 DESIRE

$1+7 = 8$ $\qquad\qquad 1+2 = 3$ 11 Desire

$1+5+6+5 = 17$ $\qquad\qquad 1+6+5 = 12$

A		E	O	E		A		O	E
1		5	6	5		1		6	5

S A L V E T O R E (N) S T A L L O N E

Remember: Always reduce all numbers to the smallest total, except when the numbers add to 11 or 22, the master numbers. Never reduce the Desire, Resource, or the Expression numbers when they add up to a master number.

ALPHA 6

THE RESOURCE

The Resource acts as a framework to produce a background for the Desire. It helps to fulfill the wishes you want from life. Your Resource works quietly within you, helping you to express yourself freely.

To arrive at the Resource, we again start with our example name. But to find the Resource, we look for the consonants this time instead of the vowels. The consonants are placed below the name.

ALPHA 7

THE CONSONANTS

```
S A L V E T O R E (N) S T A L L O N E
1   3 4   2   9     5 1 2   3 3   5
S   L V   T   R   (N) S T   L L     N
```

Note, the consonants are at the bottom of the name.

The name SALVETORE N. STALLONE has consonants of S, L, V, T, and R in the first name. It has the letter N for the middle name. The last name has S, T, L, L, and N.

If we go back again to Alpha 1 and look at the alphabet, we can again see what numbers go with which letters.

ALPHA 8

Example:

S A L V E T O R E (N) S T A L L O N E
1   3 4   2   9   5 1 2   3 3   5
S   L V   T   R   (N) S T   L L   N

1+3+4+2+9 = 19 =   5   1+2+3+3+5 = 14 = 1+4 = 5
1+9 = 10 = 1+0 = 1

The first name has numbers that add up to 1: 1+3+4+2+9 = 19 = 1+9 = 10 = 1+0 = 1. The middle name is a 5. The last name has numbers that add up to 5: 1+2+3+3+5 = 14 = 1+4 = 5. Now that this step has been completed, we can add the totals of the first, middle, and last name together.

The first name adds up to a 1. The middle name adds up to a 5. The last name adds up to a 5. Add the three together: 1+5+5 = 11. The Resource for SALVETORE N. STALLONE is 11.

ALPHA 9

THE RESOURCE

S A L V E T O R E (N) S T A L L O N E
1   3 4   2   9   5 1 2   3 3   5

1+3+4+2+9 = 19 = 1+9   5   1+2+3+3+5 = 14 = 1+4 = 5
= 10 = 1+0 = 1   5   5
     1 + 5 + 5 = 11   The Resource is 11

Alpha 10

THE EXPRESSION

The Expression is the face you present to the world. It is the side of you that is most obvious to other people whom you meet throughout your life. Your Expression shows your actions and your behavior, your talents and your capacity as you express them to the world. It includes a general assessment of your appearance, demeanor and personality.

In order to arrive at the Expression, we set up a complete row of numbers from the original name.

```
S A L V E T O R E (N) S T A L L O N E
1 1 3 4 5 2 6 9 5    5  1 2 1 3 3 6 5 5
```

1+1+3+4+5+2+6+9+5 =   5   1+2+1+3+3+6+5+5 =
36 = 3+6 = 9   5   26 = 2+6 = 8
9 + 5 + 8 = 22

The Expression for SALVATORE N. STALLONE is 22.

The Expression numbers, or the list of all numbers, will be needed later on in the building of your Alphascan 2000, but let's review our progress so far:

STEP ONE:

The Desire is the addition of the *vowels,* which are always digited on the top of the name.

STEP TWO:

The Resource is the addition of the totals of the consonants, which are always digited on the bottom of the name.

STEP THREE:

The Expression is the addition of the totals of the Desire and the Resource added together, or the list of all numbers added together.

At this point, we should review the full "understanding" of the name. When we are born, we generally receive a name and a birthdate. This is the most fundamental equipment we are given in life; this is our destiny number.

The Desire, the Resource and the Expression are the tools each of us carries with us throughout life. If one's name is changed from the birth name, it will change the person. People who change their names during their life quickly discover that their life changes as well, sometimes for the better, and other times for the worse.

It is of the utmost importance that when people change their names, the Desire, Resource, and Expression of the new name are in harmony with their birth name. This will help to explain why some people who get along just fine before marriage suddenly run into deep water after the woman takes the man's name. If her new name is not in harmony with her maiden name, the marriage could end in a divorce. In such situations, however, the Alphascan does not dictate relationships, it merely reflects what is there.

Let's look at other names for example, if your name at birth was Susan Doe. Your Desire would be 6. Your Resource would be 11. Your Expression would be 8. If your friends and your parents call you Sue, then your lifepath will change. For example, your Desire would change to 8. Your Resource would change to 1. Your Expression would change to 9. It's very important to understand the individual's full name, surname, and nicknames before doing his or her Alphascan. When there is a choice of names, pick the one by which this individual is most often and most properly identified — the name most like them.

Alpha 11

THE FOUNDATION

The Foundation is the first letter of the first name. In our example name of SALVETORE, the Foundation is the letter S, the nineteenth letter of the alphabet. This makes the Foundation for the name SALVETORE a 1, or third degree Foundation.

Example:
FOUNDATION: $S = 19 = 1 + 9 = 10 = 1 + 0 = 1$

The Foundation shows one's outlook and progress. It also shows one's mental approach as well as physical approach. The Foundation also helps you to understand the types of individuals with whom you might have to deal in your life.

Alpha 12

THE KEY OF LIFE

The Key is the addition of the first name. In our example name of SALVETORE, the Key is 9.

Example:

S A L V E T O R E
1 1 3 4 5 2 6 9 5 $= 36 = 3 + 6 = 9$

The Key of Life indicates your potential in relation to your choice of vocation. It is formed by the letter values in the first name only.

Alpha 13

THE FIRST VOWEL

The First Vowel is the first vowel that appears in the first name. In our example name of SALVETORE, the First Vowel is the letter A. If you go back to Alpha 1, you will recall that the letter A has the value of 1. The First Vowel value for SALVETORE, then, is 1.

Example:

A								VOWEL — A	
1								NUMBER — 1	
S		L	V	E	T	O	R	E	
1		3	4	5	2	6	9	5	

The letter Y is also a First Vowel in names such as Byron, Myrtle, Lynn, and Lynda; but remember Y becomes I as far as number value is concerned.

The First Vowels in our language represent the life giving force. They are of paramount importance because our First Vowels are related to the first spiritual contact with life.

Alpha 14

THE MISSING NUMBER

The Missing Numbers are the numbers that are not in the name. The Missing Numbers in the name will show what one has to work through in his or her lifetime. Let's look at our example name.

Example:

S A L V E T O R E (N) S T A L L O N E
1 1 3 4 5 2 6 9 5 5 1 2 1 3 3 6 5 5

The name has —   4 — 1's   — Letters A A S S
                  2 — 2's   — Letters T T
                  3 — 3's   — Letters L L L
                  1 — 4   — Letter V
                  5 — 5's   — Letters E E E N N
                  2 — 6's   — Letters O O
                  0 — 7's   — Missing Number . . . 7
                  0 — 8's   — Missing Number . . . 8
                  1 — 9   — Letter R
                  ——
                  18

SALVETORE N. STALLONE has 18 letters in the name. We match this total with our list of numbers and letters just so we don't miss any letters. As you can see, the name SALVETORE N. STALLONE is missing the numbers 7 and 8; again, remember these numbers represent values and qualities that the individual must come to learn in his or her lifetime.

Alpha 15

THE ABUNDANCE

The Abundance is represented by the letters that appear most often in the name. An abundance of certain numbers will indicate a strong tendency toward certain qualities, which will be seen in the answer section.

Example:

S A L V E T O R E (N) S T A L L O N E
1 1 3 4 5 2 6 9 5   5   1 2 1 3 3 6 5 5

The name has:		
	4 — 1's	— Letters A A S S
	2 — 2's	— Letters T T
	3 — 3's	— Letters L L L
	1 — 4	— Letter V
	5 — 5's	— Letters E E E N N
	2 — 6's	— Letters O O
	0 — 7's	— Missing Numbers
	0 — 8's	— Missing Numbers
	1 — 9	— Letter R

The name S A L V E T O R E (N) S T A L L O N E has an Abundance of 5, since the letter E and N are the most frequent in the name.

Example: 5 letters, E E E N N.

In the event a name has 5 fives, 5 one's, 5 nines, etc., you then add them all together:

Example: 5 fives
           5 one's
           5 nines
           15 = 1+5 = 6 Abundance = 6
(This is also done with any other combination.)

Alpha 16

THE SUBCONSCIOUS

The Subconscious shows how one will act under stress or when one is caught off guard. The Subconscious is represented by the missing numbers. For every missing number in your name, you will find it takes something away from your ability to fulfill yourself completely. To find the Subconscious, subtract the number of missing numbers from the number 9.

Example:

S A L V E T O R E (N) S T A L L O N E
1 1 3 4 5 2 6 9 5   5 1 2 1 3 3 6 5 5

	The name has:	4 — 1's	— Letters A A S S
		2 — 2's	— Letters T T
		3 — 3's	— Letters L L L
Subtract 2		1 — 4	— Letters V
From 9		5 — 5's	— Letters E E E N N
= 7		2 — 6's	— Letters O O
		0 — 7's	— Missing Numbers
		0 — 8's	— Missing Numbers
		1 — 9	— Letters R

The name is missing 2 numbers. Subtracting 2 from 9, we find we have a Subconscious of 7.

Alpha 17

THE FOUNDATION OF EXPRESSION

The Foundation of Expression shows your abilities at various levels of development. There are four ways to express yourself, or personality types, the mental, the physical, the emotional, and the intuitive.

Each Foundation of Expression also has three divisions which express behavior, the inspired, the dual and the balanced.

The Foundation of Expression is related to the determining factors of your traits, your character and your vocational possibilities. Before we learn how to arrive at your Foundation of Expression, let's find out what all these terms mean.

THE MENTAL PLANE

The mental plane will show a person how to use his or her brain power. This is the level on which a person is equipped with ideas for business and professional advancement, for writing, and for creative endeavors. Those on the mental plane have leadership qualities and inventive capacity.

THE PHYSICAL PLANE

The physical plane will show that a person is practical and energetic. People who reside in the physical plane would rather do their own work than pass it on to others. Physical activity is important to them.

THE EMOTIONAL PLANE

The emotional plane is for all creative types, for individuals whose temperaments are changeable and excitable. These people tend to let their hearts rule their brains. They care very little for facts and fail to analyze their own motives. People with artistic talent tend to reside on the emotional plane.

THE INTUITIVE PLANE

The intuitive plane is the province of the unknown and the unseen. Dwellers on the intuitive plane will have psychic and spiritual values, plus the ability to perceive mystical concepts and phenomena. This, however, is not a highly populated area.

THE INSPIRED DIVISION

When more letters are found on the inspired plane, a person will be inclined to start many things and only finish a few. Though they're always striving toward accomplishment, these individuals always seem to get side-tracked.

THE DUAL DIVISION

When more letters are found on the dual plane, a person will have a hard time making decisions. They feel themselves pulled in many directions, making it hard to come to clear-cut conclusions.

THE BALANCED DIVISION

When more letters are found on the balanced plane, a person is generally found to be very thorough and with a good character. Balance in thinking helps these individuals to know what they want out of life, and how to find it.

Alpha 17

HOW TO FIND THE FOUNDATION OF EXPRESSION

	MENTAL	PHYSICAL	EMOTIONAL	INTUITIVE
INSPIRED	A	E	ORIZ	K
DUAL	HJNP	W	BSTX	FQUY
BALANCED	GL	DM		CV

The chart above shows the alphabet and where the letters go. Take your own name and separate the letters into the appropriate blocks. Let's go to our example name of SALVETORE N. STALLONE and put the letters of the name into their proper places. S with S, A with A, L with L, and so on until we use up all the letters in the name.

Alpha 18

FOUNDATIONS OF EXPRESSION CHART

	Mental	Physical	Emotional	Intuitive	Sums
Inspired	AA	EEE	OOR		8
Dual	NN		SS TT		6
Balanced	LLL			V	4
Sums	7	3	7	1	18 = 9

After you have put the letters where they belong, add the quantity of letters in each column. First across the column, then down each column. When you reduce the total, you will find that the Foundation of Expression for the name SALVETORE N. STALLONE is 9.

Example:

Columns Across	$7+3+7+1=18$	$= 1+8 = 9$
Columns Down	$8+6+4=18$	$= 1+8 = 9$
Also: All Letters	36	$= 3+6 = 9$

When you have totalled the sums of each column, simply adding the number of letters going down and the number going across, you can begin to assess the qualities of the individual's Foundation of Expresssion. Looking at our example name, we see that SALVETORE N. STALLONE has a Foundation of Expression of 9. To understand the various sides of the 9 Foundation of Expression, consult the synopses in the Answer section of the book (Alpha 17).

To review the tendencies of this individual with regard to the Mental, Physical, Emotional, and Intuitive personalities and the Inspired, Dual, and Balanced behaviors, note which areas have the greatest number of letters and compare with the descriptions at the beginning of this section (Alpha 17).

SALVETORE N. STALLONE:

Foundation of Expression	= 9
Mental/Inspired Concentration	= 7 & 8
Emotional/Inspired Concentration	= 7 & 8

Principal characteristics for this individual will be the Emotional personality and Mental/Inspired behavior.

Answers for the Foundation of Expression are divided into either two or three trait categories, depending on the common frequency for each number. The first trait represents the highest concentration of characteristics; second and third levels are for lower concentrations of characteristics.

Alpha 19-21

FIRST CYCLE (ALPHA 19)

The first cycle is the birth month. This cycle stays in effect for the first twenty years of life; it is the cycle of formation. In these first twenty years a person will learn his or her most fundamental lessons. This is the time of life one is conditioned from home and education.

To find the first cycle, find the number for the month the person you are describing was born. Example: January is 1, February is 2, March is 3, April is 4, May is 5, June is 6, July is 7, August is 8, September is 9, October is 1, November is 11, and December is 3.

THE SECOND CYCLE (ALPHA 20)

The second cycle is the day a person is born. This cycle stays in effect from the age of twenty and it will be with a person until the end of life. This cycle is the work or vocational indicator. Throughout the years, individuals will establish themselves in the world of work and play. They will be looking at marriage and at all of life's contacts in general. To find the second cycle, write down the day the individual you are describing was born and reduce that number to its lowest digit.

THE THIRD CYCLE (ALPHA 21)

The third cycle is the year a person is born. This cycle starts at the age of fifty eight and will last until the end of life. It is the cycle of fulfillment.

In the remaining years of life a person can see his or her accomplishments, good or bad, according to how well one did during the first two cycles. It's time, in the third cycle, to realign one's life in terms of self-satisfaction. We should get rid of all aggression and develop a sense of peace and inner contentment. At this time of life, we should have a philosophy where outside conditions no longer upset our balance.

To find the third cycle, take the year of birth and reduce it to its lowest digit. Example: If the year was 1990, then reduce it: 1+9+9+0 = 19 = 1+9 = 10 = 1+0 = 1. The third cycle for the year 1990 is 1.

Alpha 22

THE GOAL

The Goal is the addition of the birth month, birth day, and birth year. During addition of the Goal, do not reduce any master numbers. The master numbers, 11 and 22, are always counted as double numbers.

The Goal works with the Expression and is one thing everyone must come to learn in life. To find a person's Goal, we total the day, month, and year of birth.

Example:

S A L V E T O R E (N) S T A L L O N E
1 1 3 4 5 2 6 9 5 5 1 2 1 3 3 6 5 5

Born: Birth Month — 11
November 26, 1990.   Birth Day — 26
                              Total — 37
                     Birth Year — 1990
     Birth Month and Day — + 37
                     Total — 2027   = 2+0+2+7=(11)

The Goal of SALVETORE N. STALLONE is 11.

Alpha 23

THE ACHIEVEMENT

There are four Achievements that work in conjunction with the three cycles. To find a person's First Achievement, add the Birth Month to the Birth Day.

To find a person's Second Achievement, add the Birth Day to the Birth Year.

To find a person's Third Achievement, add the First and Second Achievement together.

To find a person's Fourth Achievement, add the Birth Month to the Birth Year.

Example:

S A L V E T O R E (N) S T A L L O N E
1 1 3 4 5 2 6 9 5 5 1 2 1 3 3 6 5 5

Born: 11-26-1990
Reduced: 2-8-1

THE ACHIEVEMENT

First addition, the Birth Month — 2
Birth Day — 8
10 = 1+0 =
1 First Achievement

Second addition, the Birth Day — 8
Birth Year — 1
9 =
9 Second Achievement

Third addition, the addition of the first two Achievements.

The total of the First Achievement —   1

The total of the Second Achievement —   9

$$10 \quad = 1+0 = 1$$

1 Third Achievement

Fourth addition, the Birth month —   2

Birth Year —   1

$$3 \quad =$$

3 Fourth Achievement

To determine how long the First Achievement will last, subtract the Goal number from the number 36. Do not reduce any master numbers here. This will show the proper length of time the Achievements will last.

To determine how long the Second, Third, and Fourth Achievements will last, add the number 9 to each cycle.

```
S A L V E T O R E (N) S T A L L O N E
1 1 3 4 5 2 6 9 5   5   1 2 1 3 3 6 5 5
```

Born: 11-26-1990

Goal: 11

First Achievement:

Take the number   36

Subtract the goal   −11

1 year to 25 years of age.

Second Achievement:

add the number 9 to 25.

$$25$$
$$+9$$

26 years to 34 years of age.

Third Achievement:

add the number 9 to 34.

$$34$$
$$\underline{+9}$$

35 years to 43 years of age.

Fourth Achievement
add the number 9 to 43.

$$43$$
$$\underline{+9}$$

43 years to 52 years of age.

The First Achievement is of utmost importance because it is the period in which the individual obtains his or her Ego, the union of the soul and body, and sense of identity.

Your name denotes your character. Your First Cycle, Second Cycle, Third Cycle and your Goal Cycle, are the cycles that show a person how to use the resources of the name. The First Achievement, or Ego, shows how one develops during the early years. But with every Achievement there are also Demands.

Alpha 24

THE DEMANDS

There are four Demands, one for each Achievement. To find the four Demands, you must subtract all numbers instead of adding them.

To find the First Demand, subtract the Birth Month from the Birth Day. To find the Second Demand, subtract the Birth Day from the Birth Year, and to find the Third Demand, find the difference of the First and Second Demands. Finally, to find the fourth Demand, subtract the Birth Month from the Birth Year.

Example:

$$\text{Birth Date:} 11 + 26 + 1990$$
$$\text{Reduced:} 2 + 8 + 1$$

First subtraction,
the Birth Month   2
Birth Day -8

    6   = 6 = 6 First Demand

Second subtraction,
the Birth Day -8
Birth Year -1

    7   = 7 = 7 Second Demand

Third subtraction,
the difference of the   7
first two Demands. -6

    1   = 1 = 1 Third Demand

Fourth subtraction,   2
the Birth Month -1
Birth Year   1   = 1 = 1 Fourth Demand

The Achievements and Demands for our example name of
SALVETORE N. STALLONE are as follows:

First Achievement	1 . . . . First Demand	6
Second Achievement	2 . . . . Second Demand	7
Third Achievement	1 . . . . Third Demand	1
Fourth Achievement	3 . . . . Fourth Demand	1

Alpha 25

THE ALPHASCAN TIME CHART
THE ATMOSPHERE

There are four steps in building the Time Chart. The first step is the Alpha-Atmosphere. We use the first name only, each letter in the first name will last for nine years of a person's life cycle. Using the example name of SALVETORE N. STALLONE, we will use the *first name only*, SALVETORE.

Example:
S will last (9) years from the age of 1 to 9
A will last (9) years from the age of 10 to 18
L will last (9) years from the age of 19 to 27
V will last (9) years from the age of 28 to 36
E will last (9) years from the age of 37 to 45
T will last (9) years from the age of 46 to 54
O will last (9) years from the age of 55 to 63
R will last (9) years from the age of 64 to 72
E will last (9) years from the age of 73 to 81

Now, let's use the name SALVETORE but shorten it to the nickname SAL. The nickname will also have letters that will last for nine years each. You will note, after going through the three letters of SAL, the cycle repeats itself.

Example:
S will last (9) years from the age of 1 to 9
A will last (9) years from the age of 10 to 18
L will last (9) years from the age of 19 to 27
S will last (9) years from the age of 28 to 36
A will last (9) years from the age of 37 to 45
L will last (9) years from the age of 46 to 54 Etcetera.

If you wish to find the "Atmosphere" beyond age 54, continue repeating the cycle.

Alpha 26

THE ALPHA-PASSAGE

The second step in building the time chart is the Alpha-Passage, which is based on the entire name, the first, middle, and last name. Each of the passage letters travel throughout a person's life separately from each other. Let's look at how many years all the letters of the alphabet will be active.

Example:

The Alphabet:

A	J	S	Passage lasts for (1) year
B	K	T	Passage lasts for (2) years
C	L	U	Passage lasts for (3) years
D	M	V	Passage lasts for (4) years
E	N	W	Passage lasts for (5) years
F	O	X	Passage lasts for (6) years
G	P	Y	Passage lasts for (7) years
H	Q	Z	Passage lasts for (8) years
I	R		Passage lasts for (9) years

Now that you have studied how long the *letter passage* will last, we can now set up the Alpha-Passage, still using the example name of SALVETORE N. STALLONE, or your own name.

Example:

First Name

(S) will last for (1) year

(A) will last for (1) year

(L) will last for (3) years

(V) will last for (4) years

(E) will last for (5) years

(T) will last for (2) years

(O) will last for (6) years

(R) will last for (9) years

(E) will last for (5) years

Middle Name

(N) will last for (5) years

Last Name

(S) will last for (1) year

(T) will last for (2) years

(A) will last for (1) year

(L) will last for (3) years

(L) will last for (3) years

(O) will last for (6) years

(N) will last for (5) years

(E) will last for (5) years

Let's go to Alpha 27 and look at the Alpha Time Chart. It will show how the name is to be set up. You should note that the First name is on the first line. The Middle name is on the next line. The Last name is on the last line.

In setting up the Alpha-Passage, one can see that the First name, Middle name, and the Last name are all lined up under each other. This will allow us to explore what a person will be like year after year.

Let's look at the Alphascan Time Chart to see what the name of SALVETORE N. STALLONE has going for it at age 30.

Example:

The Alpha-Atmosphere   (V)

The Alpha- Passage   (R)

                               (N)

                               (L)

Alpha 27

THE ALPHASCAN TIME CHART
ALPHA — ASTMOSPHERE
ALPHA — PASSAGE

Alpha-Atmosphere

0	1	2	3	4	5	6	7	8	9	Nine year cycle
S	S	S	S	S	S	S	S	S	A	

Alpha-Passage

0	1	2	3	4	5	6	7	8	9	
S	A	L	L	L	V	V	V	V	E	The First Name
N	N	N	N	N/N	N	N	N	N/		The Middle Name
S	T	T	A	L	L	L	L	L		The Last Name

Alpha-Atmosphere

10	11	12	13	14	15	16	17	18	Nine Year Cycle
A	A	A	A	A	A	A	A	L	

Alpha-Passage

10	11	12	13	14	15	16	17	18	
E	E	E	E	T	T	O	O	O	The First Name
N	N	N	N	N/N	N	N	N		The Middle Name
O	O	O	O	O	O	N	N	N	The last Name

Alpha-Atmosphere

19	20	21	22	23	24	25	26	27	Nine Year Cycle
L	L	L	L	L	L	L	L	V	

19	20	21	22	23	24	25	26	27	
O	O	O	R	R	R	R	R	R	The First Name
N/N	N	N	N	N/N	N	N			The Middle Name
N	N	E	E	E	E	E/S	T		The Last Name

Alpha 27

THE ALPHASCAN TIME CHART
(2)

Alpha-Atmosphere

28	29	30	31	32	33	34	35	36	
V	V	V	V	V	V	V	V	E	Nine Year Cycle

Alpha-Passage

28	29	30	31	32	33	34	35	36	
R	R	R	E	E	E	E	E/S		The First Name
N	N/N	N	N	N	N/N	N			The Middle Name
T	A	L	L	L	L	L	L	O	The Last Name

Alpha-Atmosphere

37	38	39	40	41	42	43	44	45	
E	E	E	E	E	E	E	E	T	Nine Year Cycle

Alpha-Passage

37	38	39	40	41	42	43	44	45	
A	L	L	L	V	V	V	V	E	The First Name
N	N	N/N	N	N	N	N/N			The Middle Name
O	O	O	O	O	N	N	N	N	The Last Name

Alpha-Atmosphere

46	47	48	49	50	51	52	53	54	Nine Year Cycle
T	T	T	T	T	T	T	T	O	

Alpha-Passage

46	47	48	49	50	51	52	53	54	
E	E	E	E	T	T	O	O	O	The First Name
N	N	N	N/N	N	N	N	N		The Middle Name
N	E	E	E	E	E/S	T	T		The Last Name

Alpha 28

THE ALPHA ESSENCE

The third step in building the Alphascan Time Chart is the Alpha Essence. This is the addition of the nine year cycle letter that's found in the Alpha Atmosphere. It is also all the letters that are under one another in the Alpha-Passage. Looking at the example name at age 30, we see that SALVETORE N. STALLONE has an Essence of 3.

Example:

The Alpha-Atmosphere	V = 4
The Alpha-Passage	R = 9
	N = 5
	L = 3

Total 21 = 2+1 = 3 Essence.

Alpha 29

THE ALPHA AGE

The fourth step in building the Alphascan Time Chart is the Alpha Age. There is a vibration in relation to one's age. A person goes from birthday to birthday formulating a new plan of action for the year. The Alpha Age is determined by the addition of a person's age and the age the person is going into. The example of SALVETORE N. STALLONE is at the age of 30, which means he is going on 31.

Example:

Age 30 = 3+0 = 3
Age (31) = 3+1 = (4)
Total   7   = 7 Alpha Age

Alpha 30

THE ALPHASCAN TIME CHART REVIEW

The *Alpha-Atmosphere* covers a nine year span. Each letter is slower in action than those in the Alpha Passage. The Atmosphere deals with a person's inner development of character, but may also relate to any outward events that will touch a person's life.

The first two years of the letter Atmosphere will form a base for what a letter is to represent. The third year will produce your Expression; the fourth year is for a person to learn the meaning of his or her Foundation; the fifth year represents a turning point for the following years; the sixth, seventh, eighth, and ninth are the years of fulfillment of what was begun during the first year.

The Alpha Passage is a person's motivation. The letters in the name help to show a person when to make any change or when to prepare for coming events. It also shows a person how to protect their finances, health, love life, etc.

The Alpha Essence is the total experience for any given year of one's life cycle. The Alpha Essence gives an overall look at each year of life, in conjunction with the letters in force pertaining to the Atmosphere and the Passage as a whole.

The Alpha Age is the point at which a person goes from one birthday to another, formulating a new plan of action for the year.

Alpha 31

THE PERSONAL YEAR

The Personal Year is a very important factor. The Personal Year works in connection with the Alpha Passage, creating action for what a person wishes to accomplish each year of life. Personal Years are numbered 1 through 9 years. When the cycle gets to 9, it starts back again at number 1. Each Personal Year is effective from the month of January to the month of December of every year, but the Personal Year does not change on a person's birthday. To find the Personal Year, add the person's Birth Month to the Birthday. Then add the Birth Month and Day to the Universal Year. The Universal Year is the year that a person is living in at the present time — when the Alphascan is being compiled.

Example:
SALVETORE N. STALLONE
Birth Month $11 = 1+1 = 2$
Birth Day $26 = 2+6 = 8$
Universal Year 1990 = $1+9+9+0 = 19 = 1+9 = 10 = 1$

Reduced:

Birth Month   2
Birth Day   8
Universal Year   1
$$11 = 1+1 = 2$$

The Personal Year that SALVETORE N. STALLONE was born in is the Personal Year of 2. To find out what Personal Year SALVETORE N. STALLONE is going to be in in the year 1998, we make these additions.

Example:

Birth Month $11 = 1+1 = 2$
Birth Day $26 = 2+6 = 8$
Universal Year 1998 $= 1+9+9+8 = 27 = 2+7 = 9$

Reduced:

Birth Month   2
Birth Day   8
Universal Year   9
$$19 = 1+9 = 10 = 1$$

SALVETORE N. STALLONE will be in a (1) Personal Year in 1998.

Alpha 32

THE PERPETUAL (LASTING) CYCLES

Each person has seven major cycles each year of their life. These cycles are further divided into seven sub-cycles. When we remove a person's Birth Day from the year, we can then divide the year into seven fifty-two day cycles. 364 divided by 7 = 52.

To find the Perpetual cycles, start counting the days right after the birthdate. Count 52 days for the first cycle, 52 days for the second cycle, etc., until you come back to the person's birthdate. You will have a total of seven (7) complete cycles. Look under Answer Section — Achievements, 1-7.

Example:

SALVETORE N. STALLONE, Birthday: November 26.

First Cycle November	(27)	— January (17)	= Energy
Second Cycle, January	(18)	— March (10)	= Sensitivity
Third Cycle, March	(11)	— May (1)	= Expression
Fourth Cycle, May	(2)	— June (22)	= Foundation
Fifth Cycle, June	(23)	— August (13)	= Freedom
Sixth Cycle, August	(14)	— October (4)	= Adjustment
Seventh Cycle, October	(5)	— November (25)	= Perfection

Alpha 34

PERSONAL MONTH CYCLE

The Personal Month Cycle has two sub-cycles. One is the Building Cycle, which is the numbers 1, 2, 3, 4, 5. These numbers take eleven months to establish themselves. The second cycle is called the Fulfillment Cycle, which is the numbers 6, 7, 8, 9. These numbers take only nine months to establish themselves.

To arrive at the Personal Month number, add the number of the month a person was born to the Universal Year number. The Personal Month Cycle changes every year as does the Personal Year number.

Example:

SALVETORE N. STALLONE has a Personal Year number of 1 in 1998.

His birth month is 11.

Birth Month $\quad 11 = 2$

Universal Year $1998 = 1 + 9 + 9 + 8 = 27 = 2 + 7 = 9$

$\qquad 11 = 1+1 = 2$ Personal Month Cycle

YOUR PERSONAL MONTH CYCLE

ELEVEN MONTH CYCLES

Your personal cycle number is:

(1) Your personal cycle always starts in *September* and ends in *July* of the next 2nd personal year. Energy.

(2) Your personal cycle always starts in *August* and ends in *June* of the next 3rd personal year. Sensitivity.

(3) Your personal cycle always starts in *July* and ends in *May* of the next 4th personal year. Expression.

(4) Your personal cycle always starts in *June* and ends in *April* of the next 5th personal year. Foundation.

(5) Your personal cycle always starts in *May* and ends in *March* of the next 6th personal year. Freedom.

NINE MONTH CYCLES

(6) Your personal cycle always starts in *April* and ends in *December* of the same year. Adjustment.

(7) Your personal cycle always starts in *March* and ends in *November* of the same year. Perfection.

(8) Your personal cycle always starts in *February* and ends in *October* of the same year. Organization.

(9) Your personal cycle always starts in *January* and ends in *September* of the same year. Understanding.

Alpha 35

THE OCCUPATIONAL GRAPH

Certain numbers have an affinity for each other. They have compatible mathematical patterns. These patterns or groupings of three (3) numbers associated with one's birth month, day, and year are known as the Birthpath. The numbers of the Birthpath help one to better understand which vocation he or she may follow with the greatest chance of success. These numbers can be presented visually in the Occupational Graph.

To construct the Occupational Graph, begin with the birth month, day, and year, but do not use the first number of the century in the birth year. For example, in the year 1990 we use the 990 and not the 1; the 1 is eliminated for practical and mathematical reasons.

The standard chart shows the placement of the numbers and what the values represent.

Example:

THE OCCUPATIONAL GRAPH

	Personal	Group	Community	
Triangular Numbers	3	6	9	Highly Creative
Curved Numbers	2	5	8	Creative and Practical
Angular Numbers	1	4	7	Practical

Using the birth month, day, and year of our example — November 26, 1990 — the numbers will appear on the Occupational Graph as follows:

Example:

Birth Month, November	— 11		6	9,9
Birth Day	— 26	2		
Birth Year	—(1)990	11		

By looking at the standard chart above we can see that SALVETORE N. STALLONE's Occupational Graph shows that he is "highly creative" in Group and Community affairs; he is "creative and practical" in Personal affairs; and he is "practical" in his Personal affairs. In fact, the 11 in his personal affairs suggests that this individual is exceptionally gifted and mature in his business and professional life, which is represented in the Personal aspect as well.

Alpha 36

YEAR COMPARISONS

The Year Comparison is an overall look at your Alphascan 2000 as a whole. To create a model which gives a visual portrait of these aspects, we construct two sets of circles. (See the Models in the Worksheets at the back of the book.) The first column covers a period from January 1st to your birthday. The second column covers a period from your birthday to December 31st. Circles in the two columns represent, from top to bottom, Mental Approach, Field for the Year, and Physical Approach.

In the positions marked Year you write in the number for the Personal Year (Alpha 31). In the positions marked Age you write in the number for your Age from the data in the Alpha Age (Alpha 29) before birthday on the left and after birthday on the right. Obviously, you increase your Age by one year after your birthday.

In the position marked Cycle your numbers will represent the addition of the Goal number (Alpha 22) to the Atmosphere number (Alpha 25). The position marked Method is the addition of your present Achievement number (Alpha 23) to your Essence number (Alpha 28).

Once you have completed all these numbers and placed them on the Year Comparisons Model, add the Personal Year and Age digits and place the sum (reduced to its lowest value)

YEAR COMPARISONS

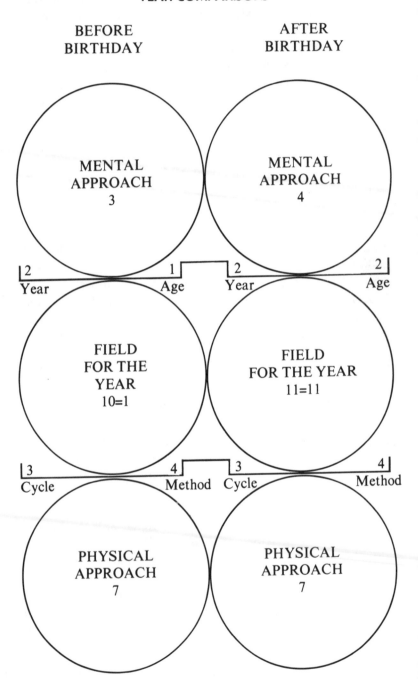

BEFORE
BIRTHDAY

AFTER
BIRTHDAY

MENTAL
APPROACH
3

MENTAL
APPROACH
4

2
Year

1
Age

2
Year

2
Age

FIELD
FOR THE
YEAR
10=1

FIELD
FOR THE YEAR
11=11

3
Cycle

4
Method

3
Cycle

4
Method

PHYSICAL
APPROACH
7

PHYSICAL
APPROACH
7

in the upper circles, labeled Mental Approach. The Before and After Birthday sums will be different.

Next, add the Cycle and Method numbers and place the sums in the bottom circles, labeled Physical Approach. Again, be sure these numbers are reduced to their lowest value.

The number in the middle circles, labeled Field for the Year, is arrived at by adding all four numbers around the circle — Year, Age, Cycle and Method in the column Before Birthday; and Year, Age, Cycle and Method in the column After Birthday. If the sum of these numbers is a Master Number, 11 or 22, leave these numbers unreduced; all other large numbers should be reduced to their lowest value. The number 10, for example, reduced to 1 while the Master Number 11 remains the same.

The Year Comparisons Model constructed in this way gives a quick review of the principal aspects of your Alphascan 2000 before and after your birthday.

Alpha 37

THE ELEMENTS

When you are making further deductions about a name, you should learn something of the Elements behind each number. On occasion you may be confronted with the question, "Will I get along with this man or this woman? Should we get married? Will our love last? Will this person be a good friend in business? Will this man or woman be right for a partnership?" All these questions and more can be answered simply by comparing the Elements.

When comparing Elements, we begin by considering each person's Desire to see if it is compatible with the other person's. Next we consider the Expression, to see if it is compatible, then we consider the Second Cycle.

The four elements are Fire, Earth, Air, and Water, four basic components of matter, first conceived of in medieval philosophy, and which provide a convenient analogy for the applications of number science as we will apply them in the Alphascan 2000. The numbers associated with these Elements are Fire — 1, 3, 9; Earth — 4, 6, 8; Air — 5, 6, 11; Water — 2, 7, 22. The number 6 is both Earth and Air. Now let's look at what compares with what.

Example:

Fire and Fire is too forceful

Fire and Earth will unlock (disciplinary)

Fire and Air will unlock (air fans flame)

Fire and Water is powerful and explosive

Earth and Earth, too slow and too material

Earth and Air, not adapable at all

Earth and Water, very congenial, mixes well

Water and Water, very static, introspective

THE MEANING OF THE NUMBERS

Fire / 1 — Energy, activity, change as related to the individual

3 — Creativity, expression with voice, pen, tools

9 — Universal approach, understanding of humanity

Earth / 4 — Personal service, application, endurance

6 — Service to community and groups, practical helpfulness

8 — Organizational, productive

Air / 5 — Understanding of life, freedom to investigate

6 — Devotion to duty, group creativity

11 — Spiritual uplift, idealism, vision

Water / 2 — Concerned with emotions and reactions, imaginative

7 — Searches for truth, analyzes motives

22 — Permeates all worlds and planes; produces constructive activity

Alpha 38

THE YEARLY ACHIEVEMENTS

The Yearly Achievements are a quarter breakdown of how you will live during any given month throughout the year. This cycle will change every year of your life. After you have found your personal achievement numbers, go to the Alphascan 2000 section titled, Alpha 23 Answers. To find your achievements, add your Birth Month to your Birth Day and add that to your Personal Year.

Example:

$$S A L V E T O R E (N) S T A L L O N E$$
Born: 11 — 26 — 1990
Reduced: 2 — 8 — 1 — Personal Year 2

THE ACHIEVEMENT

First addition, the Birth Month	2	
Birth Day	+8	
	10	= 1+0 = 1

Second addition, the Birth Day	8	
Personal Year	+2	
	10	= 1+0 = 1

Third addition, the addition of the first two Achievements.

The total of the first Achievement	1	
The total of the second Achievement	+1	
	2	= 2

Fourth addition, the Birth Month   2
             Personal year $\underline{+2}$
                             4 = 4

The First Achievement is 1, it will last through January, February, March

The Second Achievement is 1, it will last through April, May, June

The Third Achievement is 2, it will last through July, August, September

The Fourth Achievement is 4, it will last through October, November, December

The Personal Goal number is 3. It is obtained as follows:

Birth Month	2
Birth Day	8
Personal Year	$\underline{+2}$
	12 = 1+2 = 3

You can do the same thing with each day of your life, the day is broken down the same way as the year, except that it pertains to portions of the day. The First Achievement lasts from 11 p.m. to 5 a.m. The Second Achievement lasts from 5 a.m. until 11 a.m. The Third Achievement lasts from 11 a.m. until 5 p.m. The Fourth Achievement lasts from 5 p.m. until 11 p.m.

Example:

First Achievement	11 p.m.	to	5 a.m.
Second Achievement	5 a.m.	to	11 a.m.
Third Achievement	11 a.m.	to	5 p.m.
Fourth Achievement	5 p.m.	to	11 p.m.

Alpha 39

RULERSHIPS FOR PARTS OF THE BODY

From your personal number:

1. *Head* — The number 1 relates to all parts of the head. Ideas (1) begin in the mind and project themselves to all parts of the body. The planet Mars and the Element Fire are related to the head and the beginning of action.

2. *Kidneys* — Absorption (2) and elimination of waste are the principal functions of the kidneys. The Moon and Water create fluctuations in the body and establish the elemental relationship to this cleansing process.

3. *Throat-Liver* — Expression (3) comes through the throat and voice mechanism. Because the liver secretes bile and creates changes in the bloodstream, this organ is also implicated in our exercise of expression. The liver is also regarded (especially by European cultures) as the seat of desire, such as amorous urges. For this reason, the number 3, ruled by Venus-Mercury, and its Element of Fire, is associated with physical love and the expression of love.

4. *Bony Structures (teeth, joints, etc.), Abdominal Region, Circulation* — As the basis (4) for all bodily activity, Saturn and Earth represent the building requirements to keep the body healthy. Calcium is the essential nutrient of teeth and bones. Saturn also impairs or delays blood circulation. Lack of proper circulation produces infection. The stomach or digestive cavity (4) absorbs food in the early digestive stages. Teeth (4) masticate food so that it is easily absorbed through the stomach. It is simple to understand why worry (4) will create stomach disorders.

5. *Nerves, Sex Organs* — Nerves are linked to the physical

impulses of the body. The tension of the number 5 — Mars, air — causes strain on the nervous system. Number 5 ("center" of man) represents sensation as applied to the nerve center impulses. The desire for physical activity and procreation is stimulated by the ever-active, ever-seeking sensory quality of 5. When the physical desires are blocked or frustrated, the nervous system is taut and strained to the breaking point.

6. *Heart, Spine* — The heart, by contracting rhythmically, keeps up the circulation of the blood. Jupiter, ruler of 6, distributes or expands blood to the proper body parts. The spine, in which the spinal cord is situated and from which all nerves extend, occultly represents the Kundalini. The Kundalini raises the lowest forces of the body to their highest potentials connecting the adrenal glands at the base of the spine to the pituitary gland at the base of the brain. The number 6 and Jupiter rise consciousness to its highest levels. Heart and spine must work in perfect coordination to adjust (6) body functions.

7. *Intestines (elimination — congestion)* — Neptune ruled, the number 7 may be related to blockage in the intestinal tract. Proper elimination is vitally important. The number 7 may confuse diagnosis, especially in 7 Personal Year or 7 Essence. Congestion in the bloodstream may also take place with this number.

8. *Stomach, Solar Plexus* — Saturn-ruled 8 represents the balance of power necessary for bodily health. The solar plexus, lying in the direct center of the body (near the stomach), is occultly considered as the point of power (8) from which all life force flows. Tension and strain (8) react through the stomach. All fixed or set conditions (Saturn) are attributed to 8.

9. *Sex Organs, Inflammation, Emotional Reflexes* — The intensity of 9, ruled by the Sun, affects the body through the emotions. Inflammation — manifested by redness and swelling, with heat and pain — is the culmination of all the forces from numbers 1 through 9. Emotion, in its lower forms, is associated with sex urges.

Alpha 40

COLORS

Colors are represented by the spectrum or rainbow. Frequently the spectrum is shown as an arc, though it is in reality a circle. We see it as an arc because the earth's horizon cuts the rainbow at its mid-point. The seven colors of the spectrum, properly blended, produce the purest white, the highest vibration, and the color accorded the greatest spiritual significance. The absence of white, or light, means the absence of all color, or black. Black is known to absorb the most light — it is the symbolic color of ignorance, or Satan (Saturn), according to the ancients. Darkness (black) is associated with the disciplinary force of Saturn.

1. *RED* — Mars the activator is always represented by the first primary color due to its forcefulness and aggressiveness. (Element: fire)

2. *ORANGE* — is the mediator between 1 and 3 (blend of red and yellow) — represents the fusion of "two-ness" of the Moon ruler. (Element: water)

3. *YELLOW* — The second primary color is the expression of the creative trinity life — joy — strength. Its artistic side is shown by Venus and its intellectual side by Mercury. (Element: fire)

4. *GREEN* — is the manifestation or form for future expression. Its blend of yellow and blue makes it neither warm or cold. It is Saturn in its constructively secure aspects. (Element: earth)

5. *TURQUOISE* — The ever-moving, restless seeking is denoted by the changeable green-blue blend of this color. This airy Mars is a contract to the fiery Mars of 1. (Element: air)

6. *BLUE* — The third and last primary color, blue, is known as the universal color. It is deep, vital and balanced. It is soothing, tranquil, the sign of service and fidelity as indicated by its ruler Jupiter. (Elements: earth and air)

7. *VIOLET* — This is the last color of the spectrum — a blend of red and blue. It is the color of the mystic (Neptune) — subdued, grave, spiritual. It acts as a sedative. (Element: water)

8. *ROSE* — is a higher vibration of red — power at its most balanced. Saturn ruled, it is disciplined and kingly. (Element: earth). Black is also assigned to 8.

9. *GOLD* — is wisdom, glory — epitome of all colors — giver of life — the Sun. (Element: fire)

11. *PLATINUM* — or silver — the sparkle of Uranus, its ruler. (Element: air)

22. *COPPER* — or red-gold — it is the light of the sun mixed with the red clay of the earth. It adds a burnished quality to Pluto its ruler. (Element: water)

Wear the color of your Desire for relaxation, of your Resources for security, of your Expression to assert your capabilities, of your Goal to attract new opportunities, of your Second Cycle for professional advancement, of your personal years, months and days to meet the circumstances represented by each number.

THE ALPHASCAN 2000 ANSWERS

The following section provides the answers and interpretations for the systems and principles presented in the first half of the book.
For simplicity, the worksheets at the back of the book provide a place to record your numbers, page references, and other notes.

Alpha 3

THE DESIRE

1 Desire — You will start many things in life and will only finish a few of them. You like to take the lead when it comes to your surroundings. You also wish to give your ideas to others, sometimes too quickly. You have valuable ideas and should learn to use them properly within yourself. There is a desire to express your individuality. Always be sure to express yourself well in everything you do.

2 Desire — You like peace and harmony in your life. You may have a battle within yourself when you feel that you're in situations you cannot face. You can lose a lot through your inability to reach clear-cut and quick decisions.

3 Desire — You like to be attractive to other people and most of all the opposite sex. You desire recognition for your talents. You also have a desire to be the center of attention at times. Do not become self-centered; share your ideas with others. You are a creative person, which will help you throughout life. Always look for pleasant surroundings. Do not over-express yourself to the point of boring other people.

4 Desire — You are unhappy without a home. You have a need to be loved, and you like helping other people. You desire security above all things in your life. You feel incomplete if you have no one to help in life. You're a person who must create your own security. This can be done by utilizing all your inner resources and doing your work conscientiously in any group in which you function. Try not to follow along traditional life patterns, but if you feel you must, then at least try some new methods to add appeal and variety to your life.

5 Desire — You're a person who needs the freedom to live life as you see fit. You like people and can sometimes become very enthusiastic about them and their ideas. But should you lose interest in something, you're off without explanation or apology to a new and more exciting enterprise. You have a knack for looking at life from every angle. "Rules" you don't have time for. Routine is out and too many details make you nervous.

6 Desire — You like knowing what's going on in every phase of your life. You demand responsibility from others. Your home is your castle. You have a strong desire to give advice and are sympathetic to other people. You give a lot of love to others, but you also demand love in return. You love harmony, comfort, and beauty. This is what keeps you happy.

7 Desire — Perfection is your main goal in life. You have a desire to get right to the bottom of things. You dislike facing reality so you prefer building a world of your own. You get your strength through spiritual development, but are sometimes snobbish and untouchable and you have escapist tendencies from life. You are also a shy person.

8 Desire — You are a person who likes organization. You like work that accumulates power for your inner self so you can show the world your achievements. When it comes to putting your ideas across to people, you do so with courage, strength, and determination.

9 Desire — When it comes to helping people, you are the first one to step forward. You're always looking for some way to help humanity, but at times you don't have faith in yourself when it relates to the universe. One of your main concerns in life is love. Your love is of the personal type, one on one. If you should find that your love for another has become an impersonal one, your life turns to emotional turmoil.

11 Desire — You have a great vision of life. You have spiritual power when it comes to using your intuition. Your inspiration, when you are thinking constructively, always gives you the best of life. When you are thinking negatively, you get the worst out of life. Within yourself, you have a desire to tell the world what you are feeling inside, but sometimes you cannot always put it into practical terms.

22 Desire — You find it difficult to explain to other people your way of thinking. You also cannot understand why other people have such narrow viewpoints about life. You want everything you do to be done in the largest way. You are practical and more than most people, you understand the meaning of idealism.

Alpha 6

THE RESOURCE

1 Resource — You stand up for what you believe in, sometimes too quietly but firmly. You believe in courage, in fact, you know that it is one of your greatest assets. Within yourself you are looking for a specialized background that fits your outer expression.

2 Resource — The 2 Resource will help you to fulfill your outer expression. You are protected during times of troublesome circumstances. You know how to weave your way in and out of difficult conditions. Your built-in instincts will show you how to feel for others.

3 Resource — You have a gift for the spoken word, the power to write with pen, and the talent to paint with the brush. As you are already aware, with this aspect going for you, the 3 Resource will produce endless opportunities for you to capitalize on throughout your life. You have an innate social sense when it comes to self-promotion. You should always depend on a good vocabulary and proper diction.

4 Resource — You have a desire to show the world you're an individual. To establish yourself you must work precisely, diligently, and authoritatively. You're a very dependable and loyal person to those whom you work with and love. You will find at times that other people will impose upon you to do minor duties for them. Be content to give help but always try to show other people to meet their own responsibilities as you have learned to meet yours. Always be dependable, no matter what you may relinquish in life.

5 Resource — Within yourself you know how to meet the changing conditions around you easily and with calmness. You know how to handle any situation that may arise cleverly and quickly. You have a great knowledge of people. Freedom is necessary for your satisfactory self-expression.

6 Resource — You find that you're always making constant adjustments in life, personal relationships being on the top of your list. You have a tendency to get yourself into personal complications. Since you have a need to express yourself to people, it is important to have a family and a well-ordered and beautiful household. Marriage may be a necessity for you.

7 Resource — You find it hard to live up to the expectations that you have for other people. You should have found that a good education is a necessity in order to fit in with the group to which you wish to belong. To find your own individuality, you must look within yourself for confidence and sustenance.

8 Resource — You have the abiity to stay with what you start, because you know you can accomplish whatever you set out to do. One of your best assets is your self assurance. Your inner power for organization will lead you to success.

9 Resource — You have unlimited potential for helping others. You have a great depth and understanding for counseling others on difficult aspects of their lives. You're always overcoming many obstacles throughout life. Your perseverance helps you to help others with their problems.

11 Resource — Because of your originality and creativity, you are able to direct your intuition into the proper channel for a better life. Do not escape from reality, but always withdraw from people that try to drain your energies.

22 Resource — You have within yourself all the resources and potentials anyone would ever need in their lifetime. Your mental reserve gives you all the strength one needs during the crises which may arise in life. You know how to handle large scale problems and reduce them to where they make sense.

Alpha 10

THE EXPRESSION

1 Expression — Because you are always trying to stay ahead of life's wheel, you sometimes forget the sensitivities of others. You have a dominant attitude, you're a born promoter, a leader of people and a pioneer. Always employ yourself where an original type of leadership is necessary.

2 Expression — One of your natural rhythmic senses is to keep peace and order in your life. You like efficiency and precision. You like to counsel other people, to establish peace diplomatically within their hearts.

3 Expression — Constructively thinking, you can sell yourself to the world. When you're thinking negatively you couldn't sell yourself to a cat, even with a hand full of fish. You are a lovely, charming and gracious person, but at times you're a time waster, going from one thing to another. Most of the time you're extremely quiet in speech and manner, and you tend to have a facility for writing, speaking, singing, and drawing. When you are thinking destructively, you will go to extremes to attract attention.

4 Expression — You're a cautious person, but you should never let your caution get in the way of your thinking. Sometimes you let your responsibilities get in the way, such as when it comes to taking steps to make progress. You should try not to be too demanding of yourself or other people, but you naturally seek to plan your life like a builder's blueprint and stay with the pattern you start. Learn to be flexible.

5 Expression — You know how to sell yourself. Because of your enthusiasm, which is your major asset, your ideas are almost always worth hearing about. You're a quick-thinking person who likes meeting interesting people. You like to travel even if it is just down the road and back. When it comes to talking, you're a very bright speaker. You're a "jack of all trades" and may be master of a few. You should always try to add variety and color to your life.

6 Expression — You are mostly concerned with the problems of other people. It upsets you when you find people who just won't help themselves. You believe in the education of the world. You do not always like the laws of your country and if you had the power to change some of them, you would. You like to give aid and assistance to others, to train young people and help the older ones.

7 Expression — Because of your scientific and investigative mind, you should always think before you act and perfect before you produce. You enjoy people who are very high in the mental and spiritual way of thinking. You are a born analyst. You'll work best in life in the research and technical fields.

8 Expression — You are not concerned with the minor problems of life. You concern yourself with the bigger issues around you. When you want something done, it's to be done rapidly and efficiently. Your speech is direct, organized and distinct. You believe that there isn't anything too big for you to handle; and if it is too big, you wouldn't admit to it anyway.

9 Expression — You have a creative Expression. You should have a good understanding of human nature. Even though you keep your tolerance within yourself, always remember to express a positive viewpoint about life. Negative thinking causes you to go back within yourself and hide instead of reaching outward for new inspiration. Constructively, you're kind, considerate and thoughtful. Let your inner emotions flow outward to others for a better understanding of life.

11 Expression — You enjoy sharing what you have learned in your daily life with other people, but you express yourself easier through lecturing, teaching, or counseling. When you think positively, everything is clear around you. Your outlook in life is a beautiful and constructive one. When you are thinking negatively, things become fuzzy, your facts get confused and it's hard to express yourself to others. Thinking negatively allows you to become erratic and unpredictable.

22 Expression — Your world and where you can function are endless. You understand how life really works. Because you can take any facts and bring them down to their real substance, you prefer to work in large enterprises. You enjoy international affairs. Sometimes the power of your own Expression causes you to be overly demanding. At times you feel you're always making allowances for other people with less vision than you. You have a special gift in life that will help to ensure that you'll never lose touch with the broad and all-encompassing perspectives of this planet.

Alpha 11

THE FOUNDATION

1 Foundation — (A) You are a very strong-minded person. You always like to be doing something and rarely worry about the outcome of what you are doing beforehand. You are always anxious to do things here and now because you have a constant stream of ideas and an abundant supply of energy.

(J) You are not overly direct or overly sure of yourself. You take life with ease. You are content with minor activity. You have a "shall I" or "shall I not" attitude.

(S) You have an intense nature. You should learn to centralize your emotions and use them in a creative way. You have a problem with your emotions. You don't know where to turn to express your inner self.

2 Foundation — (B) You pick up information around you very quickly. You enjoy giving love as much as receiving it, but you are not very selective, at times, with your friendships. You attract the strays of life who are looking for emotional security. You want other people to listen to your problems, which may already be apparent to others. You are easygoing on the outside but stubbornly tenacious inside.

(T) You're a person who must put aside your personal ambitions in order to live in the greater world of service to others.

You are a person who is secretive and who likes to probe into the mystical and psychic matters of the universe. You're always trying to gather information on the unknown and unseen world. You are always taking on more responsibility than you can handle comfortably. You are easygoing on the outside, but you are very emotional on the inside.

3 Foundation — (C) You gravitate toward other people in your desire to understand them both inwardly and outwardly. You have a natural intuition that's always producing a never ending stream of ideas.

(L) You have good mental balance, you're a practical person, a serious type of person, and you have a creative outlook on life.

(U) You are torn between the intellectual and emotional side of your character. You have hidden psychic qualities stored within you, but because of your indecision, you tend to waste your advantages instead of retaining them. Because of your moods, you may jump into sudden outbursts and quick tears. Constructively, you are very generous and you find joy in giving.

4 Foundation — (D) You are a self-contained person. You are completely content to do your work well and calmly. Your actions are slower in movement and this causes you to want to see everything in black and white before you will believe in it completely. You're a firm believer in justice which attracts confidence in people around you. You demand loyalty from your friends. It takes a long time to anger you and it takes just as long for you to forgive someone else.

(M) You're a free spirit, going to heights for the purposes of gaining freedom. You are materially minded, sometimes to the point of losing sight of what your life is all about.

5 Foundation — (E) You have a physical attraction for the opposite sex. You like being active and you're always looking for new opportunities. You have a way of changing things around you to fit your life style.

(N) You have a hard time in making your own decisions. You are too changeable in what you desire. You do have practical and usable ideas. All of your life experiences should teach you things that you won't forget easily.

(W) You like security. You don't like things to change too quickly around you; it causes turmoil. You cling to certain people, and because you do, you have a problem deciding who is important and who isn't. You do like excitement and sometimes pay a high price for that moment of enjoyment. You like outside activity and you dislike too much routine.

6 Foundation — (F) You have a compassionate sense about you and the ability to understand other people's difficulties. You respond very quickly to other people's problems and you're quick to give good advice. Your instincts react sharply and accurately.

(O) You are self-indulgent to the point that you take in anyone and everyone without much discernment. You feel guilty about your behavior when your heady enthusiasm gets you into situations too quickly. You sometimes believe you are a parent to the whole world, but you go on protecting your own interests and obsessions.

(X) You destroy yourself by always taking on more responsibilities than you should. You are too sensitive. You have a do-or-die attitude when looking after the interests of the ones you love. Anyone can depend on you and have confidence in the trust they may place in you.

7 Foundation — (G) You criticize everyone and everything, whether constructively or otherwise. You believe in getting down to the bottom of every situation the fastest way possible. You're always analyzing and diagnosing every phase of your life.

(P) You have a give-and-take attitude. You're not all that sure of yourself, and therefore you are more secretive about yourself. Because you are always getting sidetracked in life, you find it hard to carry out your original ideas.

(Y) It's always hard for you to make up your mind when you reach those crossroads of life, and you find it hard to decide which path to take for higher development or greater success. You have very good insight; why not let it show you the right direction?

8 Foundation — (H) Throughout your life, you will always keep climbing up that ladder until you get to where you wish to be. It's always a battle when you're trying to make a choice between spiritual and material matter. But you do have a good sense of what is successful and wise and what is not.

(Q) At times you have a problem trying not to step on other people's toes. Because you believe in material things for your security in life, you spend much of your time trying to gain possessions. There are times when you experience a lot of emotional fluctuations and indecision.

(Z) You have the ability within you to climb to great heights. You also have the ability to fall right to the bottom. Constructively, you have the resources of a great philosopher who believes that wisdom is the way to complete mastery.

9 Foundation — (I) Your ego is one of the most important things in your life. You can be as constructive as you wish, or you can be so destructive that you may become emotionally unbalanced. You especially like demonstrating your emotions to an audience, but you are a person who can suddenly appear to be completely impersonal, calm and outgoing.

(R) You are concerned with material values. You are a good organizer when it comes to facts and ideas. You understand the problems of other people who are more limited in life. You usually do something to help others, but in a practical way.

11 Foundation — (K) You have pure, inspired intuition. You are always open and receptive to any new ideas. You are a private person, yet you are also so revealing about yourself. You enjoy helping those who have not been as fortunate as you. When you are thinking negatively, you lose coordination in every department of your life. You will experience many ups and downs and poor feelings.

22 Foundation — (V) You have a way of judging other people and other situations insightfully and accurately. On the constructive side, you have limitless understanding. You have an exceedingly broad outlook on life and a wealth of spiritual resources on which to draw.

Alpha 12

THE KEY OF LIFE

1 Key — *1, 4, 7* — You will do your best around people who have birth dates that digit to the numbers 4 or 7. Example birth dates: 4, 13, 22, 31 as well as birth dates of 7, 16, 25. With a Key of 1 you can depend on expanding your individuality and you should apply it to any type of vocation that you may follow.

2 Key — *2, 5, 8* — You will do your best around people who have birth dates that digit to the numbers 5 or 8. Example birth dates: 5, 14, 23 and 8, 17, 26. With a 2 Key you're usually calm in your approach to life, but you're too much of a fuss budget when it comes to carrying out unimportant plans. You may also lose a lot in life because at times you cannot see the forest for the trees.

3 Key — *3, 6, 9* — You will do your best around people who have birth dates that digit to the numbers 6 or 9. Example birth dates: 6, 15, 24 and 9, 18, 27. With a 3 Key you have social qualities. It is very important to expand throughout life by constantly contacting other people. You should always employ your talents in a creative field. Because you have so much physical energy, you need to do work that requires coordination of hands and mind.

4 Key — *4, 1, 7* — (Be certain this key doesn't add up to 22.) You will do your best around people who have birth dates that digit to the numbers 1 or 7. Example birth dates: 1, 10, 19, 28 and birth dates 7, 16, 25. With a 4 Key you do your best work when you systematize your efforts. You have a great sense of precision and a desire for accuracy with anything you decide to undertake.

5 Key — *5, 2, 8* — You will do your best around people who have birth dates that digit to the numbers 2 or 8. Example birth dates: 2, 11, 20, 29 and the birth dates 8, 17, 26. With the 5 Key you have a live-and-let-live approach to life. You don't prefer to sit in judgment of others. You have an open mind when it pertains to life and you'll try anything once, so long as it makes sense to you.

6 Key — 6, 3, 9 — You will do your best around people who have birth dates that digit to the numbers 3 or 9. Example birth dates: 3, 12, 21, 30 and the birth dates 9, 18, 27. With the 6 Key you're a born artist. You're good at writing, painting and public speaking. You prefer to work around people like yourself before you go into the world at large. You have a natural-born creative mind.

7 Key — 7, 1, 4 — You will do your best around people who have birth dates that digit to the numbers 1 or 4. Example birth dates: 1, 10, 19, 28 and 4, 13, 22, 31. With a 7 Key you have a natural gift of getting right to the core of any problem, you're always probing. You're always developing new ideas and you organize, revise, reject, and reassemble those ideas until they're a perfect pattern. You also have a problem when you are negative, in that you become too literal, too critical, and too mystical.

8 Key — 8, 2, 5 — You will do your best around people who have birth dates that digit to the numbers 2 or 5. Example birth dates: 2, 11, 20, 29 and 5, 14, 23. With the 8 Key you enjoy working with cooperative enterprises and you always attract new contacts. You have a great belief in your own qualifications to meet other people easily and with diplomacy.

9 Key — 9, 3, 6 — You will do your best around people who have birth dates that digit to the numbers 3 or 6. Example birth dates: 3, 12, 21, 30 and 6, 15, 24. With a 9 Key you were born ready for action. You know how to give of yourself because you are a creative person. You need an outlet for your emotions. You can find your outlet by dealing with people in large groups.

11 Key — 1 through 9 — You will do your best around people who have birth dates that digit to the numbers 1, 2, 3, 4, 5, 6, 7, 8, 9. You will *not* do your best around people with birth dates that do not digit: these birth dates are 11 or 22. With an 11 Key, you're a penetrating person, able to prepare yourself to meet any problem which may arise. You must adapt quickly to all changing circumstances around you, and always be ready to give knowledge to those who ask for it.

22 Key — 1, 4, 7 — You will do your best around people who have birth dates that digit to the numbers 1, 4, or 7. Example birth dates: 1, 10, 19, 28, and 4, 13, 22, 31, and 7, 16, 25. With a 22 Key you can function with anyone you wish. You're a generous person but sometimes you're too expansive. You have a wealth of understanding and compassion. You should never be too objective when giving advice; use your intuition.

Alpha 13

THE FIRST VOWEL

A — First Vowel — Your approach to life is stimulating and very interesting. You're extremely direct in your manner. If you have two vowels in your name such as AI or AU, etc, you'll sense fluctuation in your feelings. You'll be more emotional and may be too quick with your personal reactions toward others.

E — First Vowel — You should have great energy along with your nervous reactions. You're a straightforward, versatile and tireless person. On a less positive side, you're determined to change things around you to suit your own purpose.

I — First Vowel — When you're being "positive," you're a dynamically and passionately creative person. There are no halfway measures in your life, being the intensely human and generous person that you are. When you are in a "negative" mood, you can be extremely cruel. You're quietly energetic and most unpredictable in your actions. "Negative" thinking allows you to suffer from inner doubts and instability, which you should try to avoid.

O — First Vowel — You are a very protective person, dedicated to love, life, and the pursuit of happiness. You have a knack for understanding other people's problems. You like the accumulation of material things. You're always dealing with family emotional uprisings which may cause you some problems, due to the fact that you're an emotional person yourself.

U — First Vowel — Your emotions get in the way of thinking. You find some difficulty in making decisions, but you're basically a generous and giving person.

Y — First Vowel — This is a vowel that, in many names, is to be judged with the vowel just ahead of it, such as AY, EY, IY, OY, UY. The letter Y, when used with another vowel, puts a spiritual overlay on the corresponding vowel. You're a spiritual person. Your insight helps you find the right direction to go in life. When major or minor problems arise, you have a hard time making up your mind in a hurry. You have a give and take outlook on life. When used by itself, as in Byron or Lynda, the letter Y behaves like the letter I and assumes the qualities of I.

Alpha 14

THE MISSING NUMBER

1 Missing Number — Sometimes you're too meek and mild. Other times you assert yourself too much. There is a need to arrive at some agreeable balance. Strive to be quietly determined in all your actions. Think out all of your actions and ideas until they take shape, before you reveal them to others. Concentrate on "first things first."

2 Missing Number — You need to learn the lessons of tact, cooperation, and consideration. You need to pay more attention to the minute-by-minute details which are always sliding by you. Learn how to say the right things at the right time so you don't overplay your hand. Remember, there's a place for everything and everything has its place.

3 Missing Number — You need to learn to listen more than you talk. You may have some difficulty in speaking when you want to impress others. You make some people resentful of your forwardness. There may also be difficulty in having children of your own. If there is a strong need to fulfill your parenting instincts, consider adopting a child. You'll have problems with love affairs or with children.

4 Missing Number — You have some confusion about the issues that confront you in life. Unless you apply yourself to a given task at a given time, you will find it difficult to secure a firm foundation in life. Learn how to save consistently, but don't be tempted to hoard in one direction and fritter away resources in another. You could be penny wise and pound foolish.

5 Missing Number — Because you resist change you will tend to overlook benefits that come your way. You shy away from the normal contacts that are necessary in your daily life. You discourage curiosity, you resist change. Your life experiences may often seem to be of the less constructive type.

6 Missing Number — You will have to make many adjustments to life. You will find marriage more than an average hurdle. You give advice where it is least desired and you fail to make allowance where it counts the most. You will misjudge your personal contacts. Your ideas are often one-sided, especially with family relationships and close ties.

7 Missing Number — You accept the surface appearances of things too quickly. You do not take time to reason out your problems sensibly. You lack true spiritual awareness during your first twenty-five years of life. Learn to stay with what you start. Learn to accept criticism graciously. You need to be more selective in all of your relationships.

8 Missing Number — You have a desire for material gain and, at the same time, a conflicting desire for material freedom. You mismanage your finances and affairs by thinking money must be spent as quickly as it is earned. You need to learn to balance all areas and resources in your life.

9 Missing Number — You have a desire to help others with their emotional problems, but you're never quite sure how to help. You tend to focus on one-on-one relationships and to ignore the world around you. You know how you feel on the inside but you can't always project it outside yourself. You are often intense and self-centered.

Alpha 15

THE ABUNDANCE

1 Abundance — You have a lot of independence. Sometimes you're too overbearing or too forceful. To be a leader, you must always have self-confidence. This will help to make sure that your ideas are understood properly and used to their best advantage.

2 Abundance — You worry too much about incidental details. You're always getting yourself tied up in knots with the little petty affairs of life. You need to be willing to rise above the small problems of life in order to focus on the greater world around you. Stop staring at the ground and start looking at the sky.

3 Abundance — You have a good imagination. You dramatize your life through your natural gift of expression. You're an attention-getter, which is the reason you can sell your ideas so easily. When you're not able to use your natural born expression, you will feel frustrated. You can find an emotional outlet by writing, painting, speaking, acting, etc.

4 Abundance — You spend a good deal of time on routine work. You have the power of mind to concentrate. Your good sense of value helps you to acquire things that have durability and substance, but you should not hang on to tradition too strongly. There is a need to ease up. Your thinking and actions tend to be inflexible. You need to learn flexibility.

5 Abundance — You have a tendency to be a changeable,

impulsive and spontaneous person. You love variety, gaiety, and you thrive on excitement. You investigate everything to learn how to improve the various phases of your daily work. You're an interesting and stimulating person to those you meet for the first time. Facts intrigue you and travel broadens your outlook.

6 Abundance — You're the type of person who will assume your responsibilities without question. However, you can be stubborn and unyielding in your ideas, and have a tendency to be too self-righteous and opinionated. When you control these instincts, you are perceptive, generous and benevolent. You will be inclined to enter community affairs because of your desire to protect others' interests.

7 Abundance — You have a love for research and a desire to probe into underlying causes. When you think negatively, you can become involved in secret dealings. But you can use your investigative and analytical skills to great advantage if you direct your thinking to positive issues.

8 Abundance — Because of your natural executive ability, you may be overly anxious for success and attainment. You believe in making things pay. You know how to get things done with dispatch, but you may be entirely too demanding, with your self-made authority. You enjoy the feeling of impressing others.

9 Abundance — You are as extreme in your generosity as you are in your emotions and behavior. Because of your charm and enthusiasm, you require an audience both professionally and privately. You should not waste your life on trivial and temporal pursuits. Proper control of your emotions and behavior are essential for happiness in your life.

11 Abundance — You have a strong inclination to be impatient with other people and you don't pay enough attention to tact and detail. You are eccentric, imaginative and psychic. You need to understand that cooperation is essential in every phase of life, especially for someone with your gifts.

22 Abundance — You have a greater vision of life than most people. You are able to perceive the universal, timeless qualities of life, of the people around you, and of day-to-day events. You should use your skill and understanding to help others.

Alpha 16

THE SUBCONSCIOUS

2 Subconscious — You want to attract attention and you don't care how you do it; but no matter how you go about it, you'll be sufficiently obvious. You will have some problems with sexual matters; you'll have a more than normal interest in experimentation.

3 Subconscious — You spend too much time on non-essentials. When your view of life gets to be non-constructive, you worry about superficial things. Because you limit your outlook on life, you tend to have great difficulty attaining success. For you to get ahead in life, you must learn to dispose of petty routine and broaden your perspectives.

4 Subconscious — You will experience inner dissatisfaction and restlessness during the first twenty years of your life. It is difficult for you to reach decisions quickly. You may want personal freedom at any cost, especially if you're missing the holding numbers of 2, 4, 6, and 8.

5 Subconscious — You feel a need for adjustments in your immediate surroundings and in your work. You also feel you must show others what to do and how to do it. The most important people to you are the ones you love and the ones you serve.

6 Subconscious — You may be insensitive, aloof, or indifferent to what is going on around you. You need to complete and perfect what you start, and to develop an analytical sense. You have faith in your own abilities. You shouldn't have fear of your future: wait for things to come to you instead of pursuing them too forcefully.

7 Subconscious — You refer everything you do to reason. In every aspect of your life, you'll be a methodical and practical type of person. You know how to execute your plans promptly and efficiently. You believe in doing things here and now, instead of waiting for future developments. You have a strong desire to make things pay.

8 Subconscious — Because you have been through so many phases of life, you are ready for a higher level of experience. You are not enthusiastic about any one thing in life, you have a tendency to generalize everything; sometimes you feel life is a bore. If you back down too quickly when challenged, you'll find the arrogance of your indifference will lead to heated discussions and arguments.

ALPHA 17

THE FOUNDATION OF EXPRESSION

1 Foundation of Expression

You are anxious for progress. You need a clear thinking process. You have self confidence and the ability to create change, but you should realize that not all new plans and new beginnings are always permanent nor always brought to a proper conclusion.

Because your mind is always becoming diverted from its purpose, you seldom rest long enough in one spot. You start many things but at times you let yourself go all the way to the bottom of life before you can see the true goal that you're trying to attain. You suffer from emotions, change, disruption, and nervous tension.

2 Foundation of Expression

You have a fear of life because you're too introverted with your feelings. Insecurity keeps you from venturing too far from home. If you don't learn to come out into the open, you will remain isolated and will fail to attain the emotional growth life holds for you. You must learn *not* to delay or defer your problems.

You're always overburdened with all the cares of the world. You should work for greater self-mastery, and learn to improve your emotional balance and mental control.

3 Foundation of Expression

You are able to see life as it really is. You understand that when you're positive you can bring out the bright, positive aspects of life. When you're negative, you become self-absorbed and fatalistic.

You're a practical and lasting type of person. You have a calm, controlled temper and a balanced attitude toward life.

You have powerful intuition; you're an open chalice of the mystic world. If you will keep your eyes and mind open, you will find that you can have all that life has to offer.

4 Foundation of Expression

You're a person who likes to work with your hands. You have a strong mental and emotional character. You prefer doing work of a physical nature. You show a practical strain with great physical endurance.

5 Foundation of Expression

When you are thinking constructively, you can cure physical and emotional ills. Positive thinking helps you to know how to balance the physical with the spiritual.

You're always looking for yourself but you seldom succeed. You're always seeking money and you always seem to find it. You like success and you generally do not care how you obtain it. On one of your more positive sides, you're the teacher who points the way to success or failure.

You are fixed mentally on security and you are able to meet any disturbance or change in life. You go to the depths or to the heights to gratify your own ambitions.

6 Foundation of Expression

You have a built-in gift which is your intuition and which you don't listen to. You become overly concerned with practical values.

If you would learn to depersonalize your emotions, you would find out that you can have everything you desire.

You need to learn when to help others and when not to. You believe in accepting your responsibilities.

You are an unknown quantity in mathematics and belong to the material side of life.

7 Foundation of Expression

You're the type of person who is thorough and practical in your deductions. You have the ability to master the sciences, to dwell on life's philosophies, to interpret all of life's laws. You know how to use wisdom in its simplest and most usable terms. After you organize your knowledge thoroughly, you supply it to others in a practical fashion.

You sometimes act as a progressive force by organizing, directing, and promoting the improvements you have perfected.

You have a sixth sense when it comes to choosing which road to take in life. You must not go from one thing to another too quickly; if you do, you tend to become scattered and defeated in your quest. Always choose the road that gives you the greatest inner peace, have patience, and have faith to stay with it until you attain your objectives.

8 Foundation of Expression

You are evenly balanced with spiritual qualities as well as material ones. At times, when you're thinking negatively, you become overloaded and lose what was so hard to gain.

You have access to the ancient symbol of fulfillment. You are spiritual, intuitive, and aware that you can bring your higher knowledge down to practical terms.

Emotions have no middle ground. You must keep your goals in sight and strive for mastery of self before you can help others with your power. You're always trying to climb the steep road to higher horizons but you must discipline yourself to understand the world around you and your inner self.

9 Foundation of Expression

You have difficulty because of your determination to think your word is law. Others just don't see it that way. You are capable of high ideals and great service to others if you could set aside your aggression and intransigence.

You have your emotions under control so you can be of help to others in need of a friend. You are a practical person who has the ability to reason while you argue, but when you get angry, you can be too demanding.

11 Foundation of Expression

There is no challenge that can be put upon you that you can't overcome. You are a master, and masters can ascend the highest height or sink to the lowest depth. There is no such thing as the word neutral when it comes to your moods. You are either incredibly happy or deeply depressed. You should always strive for perfect calm, poise, and control. You're a brilliant, sparkling type of person. When you are at your best, the electricity within you can radiate a healing light.

22 Foundation of Expression

When the spiritual quality of life is fully understood, the door is open for you to make a contribution to the world for the benefit of all mankind. You have the opportunity to understand all phases of life and you can attain spiritual fulfillment if you learn how to utilize the vision that is an integral part of you.

Alpha 19

THE FIRST CYCLE

Birth Month — The birth month cycle is in effect from the age of zero to the age of 25.

1 Birth Month Cycle — JANUARY — You are required to stand on your own early in life. You are ahead of your time. You are appreciated and yet feared. You have a warm heart but you can also be as cold as ice. You understand the real meaning of time, and you know how to prevail and win. You speak with frankness and candor when it comes to the ones you love, sometimes to the point of becoming overly possessive.

OCTOBER — You do not have much aggression and are more protected in life. You need to think for yourself and to stress individuality and self-sufficiency. You have a natural instinct for fair play, justice, and harmony. You have a lot of beauty and love within you. You may confuse emotion with logic to the point of anguish.

2 Birth Month Cycle — FEBRUARY — You are overly sensitive and may have been overly spoiled during your formative years. You were probably coddled or too protected by your mother. You need an emotional outlet away from the home environment. You are sophisticated and unique, yet on occasion you are also eccentric. You are fascinated by the new and the strange things in life. Even though you have some unorthodox methods, you're a seeker of knowledge, a seeker of adventure, and you're an individual who seeks the thrill of discovery. You need to learn the art of cooperation, and try to overcome your natural shyness. Study dancing, music, or write poetry.

3 Birth Month Cycle — MARCH — This cycle should promise a pleasant childhood; however, you scatter your abilities and jump quickly from one thing to another. All creative efforts should be encouraged. Languages and diction should be studied. If a child is left-handed, let it be; if forced to change, stuttering may result. Your emotions often dominate your logic. You are an intuitive, sensitive, and emotional person who may appear to be very quiet on the surface but may have a storm raging within you. You're a very secretive person; you never tell all you know. You can deceive others, but you also get deceived. You are artistic, musical and moody. You're also a person who is susceptible to drugs, both alcohol and other kinds. Unless you exercise discretion, you are more likely to become addicted to alcohol and drugs than most people.

DECEMBER — You should learn to be more creative rather than merely worrying about your social activities. Learn to conserve energy. You're secretive and forceful, mysterious and direct in manner. You're creative and resourceful, and a natural detective. You appreciate power, and you enjoy behind-the-scenes planning and maneuvering. Because of your curiosity, you tend to get yourself into numerous love affairs. You break most rules of life and make your own. You live life like an auto race — you have to win — and you have a way of pushing other people just as hard as you push yourself. You waste little time on the trivial things or the trivial people in the world.

4 Birth Month Cycle — APRIL — During your childhood years, you could have been restricted from a lot of things, but not necessarily through limited circumstances. Tradition may play a strong part in your life. Your parents may have been the disciplinary type to the point that your household was built on a rigid routine. You need someone whom you can look up to, someone who is daring, who has initiative, who can lead, a person who can gain your respect. You're always testing people because you're a critical thinking person. You don't like people around you who try to drain your energy or deplete your emotions. They'll find out that you know how to surprise and to contradict their next move. You're attractive, dynamic, and surprising; you're basically quiet in manner, but you have a temper that can burn the eyes out of another person. People who have learned to love you find it next to impossible to live without you. Because your goal in life is a high one, always look to the future rather than hanging on to the past.

5 Birth Month Cycle — MAY — In your youth you will look for numerous outlets for your special talents. If there are any family repressions, your inclination will be to leave the nest and venture out into the world on your own. Many changes may take place in your immediate environment. You could find yourself traveling from place to place. You are disciplined, but you should keep your physical urges intact. You're stubborn yet easygoing. There is a restlessness about you. You're always becoming involved in rumors. You can love more than one person at a time, and you're always falling in and out of love. You are always concerned with money; you don't like anything or anyone to distract you from it. Learn to be versatile; don't scatter your forces. Be determined, but appreciate the gains and profits you earn along the way.

6 Birth Month Cycle — JUNE — In your early years you may have been hovered over more than necessary. You may also have had a lot of duties and responsibilities put upon you by your family. You feel a need to belong, to give love and to be loved in return. If you had a lot of demands put upon you as a child, you will probably get married quite young. Because of your inner sense of security, you like helping others, but you're a very complex person. You're not always sure of what you want or need. You seem to get involved with people who end up hurting you. Home and homemaking are important to you. You're always building your nest, accumulating wealth, and stocking your staples. Money is important to you.

7 Birth Month Cycle — JULY — Youth is the time for your inner development through education. As a child you were probably the type who had a tendency to be secretive and introverted. You should have learned to avoid aggression and to know that your greatest opportunities come when they are not reached for — they disappear if pursued. Examine your motives, don't be over critical, and avoid aloofness. Look carefully before you undertake marriage, and, then, be very selective of your life partner. You have a drive to accumulate material goods. On the negative side, you are moody and ultra-sensitive. You have personal magnetism, but you can be obstinate and very determined in your quest for experience. The key to your success is through love, affection, and appreciation. But because of your need for love, you can be hurt easily.

8 Birth Month Cycle — AUGUST — In your growing years you'll find certain tension and strain, especially from older people. This strain can also be caused by humble circumstances. On the other hand, there may be great wealth around you with no explanation of where it came from. You have a drive for power which may make you too forceful. You'll have a desire to make a place for yourself in life which may be hard to achieve. At times you're boastful and you tend to exaggerate. You live for love and love to live. You know how to plan your life well, and you're a born trainer (educator) of other people, but because of your need for love, you open yourself up to insult and injury. You always seem to be making the wrong choices; you're always meeting the right people at the wrong time. Learn to overcome your impulsiveness.

9 Birth Month Cycle — SEPTEMBER — This could be a difficult cycle during the childhood years because life seems to you to be too big, too vague, and too unchartered. There may be some nervousness and uncertainty about you which may appear to be a hot temper, but which is only a fear of a world that you do not understand sufficiently. You are a creative person, but you need to learn to meet others comfortably. You do have a way of sizing up other people, and at times you're so outgoing and so beautiful; but at other times, you're very withdrawn. In general, you're extremely practical about anything you do. You may appear to be a health nut to the point of being fanatical about vitamins and exercise. You take life seriously. You enjoy the philosophies of great people, but you love your own philosophy the best. What is fascinating about you is your affinity for contradictions.

11 Birth Month Cycle — NOVEMBER — As a child you may find that this cycle creates nervous tensions. You'll have a tremendous dramatic sense. You will need a great deal of rest to relax from your mental and muscular exertions. Children of this cycle often have a strange imagination, and sometimes it's hard to tell the difference between a deliberate lie or fanciful thinking on their part. You may also have certain fears and phobias. You sometimes falsify the facts because of your fear of being found out. Also, you have a tendency to procrastinate. You should always do what you think is right; go out and do it instead of talking about it, and don't settle for anything but the best. You have great potential, so don't be afraid to achieve it. You like to travel; it's not always easy to pin you down. You feel that the way to an open mind is through traveling.

Alpha 20

THE BIRTH DAY CYCLE

1 Birth Day Cycle, 1-10-19-28 Birth Days — You can specialize in any field. You'll find other people will turn to you for support and encouragement. The 1 birthdays are the people who are most independent. The 10 birthdays like working with other people. When it comes to large groups, the 10s will usually take the lead. The 19 birthdays must depend on objectivity in the effort of getting ahead. The 28 birthdays always need to be cooperative when working with other people.

2 Birth Day Cycle, 2-20 Birth Days — Physicians, musicians, dancers, diplomats, charity workers, statisticians, and secretaries are frequently natives of this cycle, where service to other people is needed. You have little desire for being put into the spotlight because of your super-sensitivity, but you do wish to receive acclaim for work well done. Your love life, your home life, and the love of those near and dear are essential to your happiness.

3 Birth Day Cycle, 3-12-21-30 Birth Days — Artists, actors, designers, engineers, lawyers, physicians, singers, teachers, and writers are natives of this cycle. You should have a forceful personality and will find it's most important for your career. You tend to mix with other people comfortably.

4 Birth Day Cycle, 4-12-31 Birth Days — Architects, builders, designers, doctors, chemists, engineers, landscape artists, and technicians in all fields are native to this cycle. You love your home, so you should learn to protect your domestic relationships because love is important. Learn to show your softer side to others. Don't let your work worries affect your health. Find an enjoyable hobby or some light outside interest to get your mind off your daily routine.

5 Birth Day Cycle, 5-14-23 Birth Days — Analysts, critics, diagnosticians, explorers, lawyers, psychiatrists, psychologists, and salesmen are often born into this cycle. Do not be disturbed when you're uprooted from time to time. You'll meet your greatest opportunities in new places and among new people. Always undertake work that has many interesting angles, the type that can be done quickly and under pressure. Abuse of your natural desires will deplete the energy required for your advancement.

6 Birth Day Cycle, 6-15-24 Birth Days — Analysts, decorators, doctors, lawyers, personnel consultants, painters, general practitioners, politicians, and persons in the performing arts are in this cycle. Writers with a message, artists who interpret themselves through music, and all fields where service is accented belong here, as is anyone who has to do with homemaking. Responsibilities should be assumed but be sure to take great care to avoid any personal complications that do not concern you directly.

7 Birth Day Cycle, 7-16-25 Birth Days — Among the natives of this cycle are individuals with analytical, mental and technical outlets; lawyers, doctors, and surgeons; bankers, brokers, electrical experts, inventors, technical or philosophical educators, writers, clergymen, psychics, draftsmen, and teachers. Authorities in all professions that require analytical skills often begin here. You will find it necessary to specialize and to perfect. To retard your ambitions and potentials, keep on procrastinating. It can and will delay your progress.

8 Birth Day Cycle, 8-17-26 Birth Days — Natives of this cycle include executives, and people in banking, buying, building, consulting, manufacturing, organizing, and anything to do with big business. You know how to achieve and produce. You are often found on the organizational side of the professional occupations. Those around you recognize that you can always be trusted. You should be concerned with large scale developments.

9 Birth Day Cycle, 9-18-27 Birth Days — You work best in professions where service is accented, such as writing, painting, lecturing, teaching, medicine, law, and the ministry. Your emotions, by now, should be under control to the point that your mind can dominate your actions. You have a love for the arts, you have a good sense of color and a desire to serve others. You have a desire to travel so you can gain more understanding of other people. You may sometimes disregard or rearrange your religious values entirely until you find an answer that satisfies your own purposes. Because your business is your life's work, you cannot bear to be in a subordinate position.

11 Birth Day Cycle, 11-29 Birth Days — You belong in aviation, electronics, psychiatry, psychology, philosophy, radio, politics, television, or any advanced profession. You are a teacher par excellence. You may feel some tension in developing your ideals. You do your best work through creation, inspiration, and revelation. You should be a specialist in whatever type of work you undertake. With this cycle, you may find difficulties in marriage until you learn to be completely cooperative.

22 Birth Day Cycle, 22 Birth Days — Your career choice is a universal one. International affairs, diplomacy, large scale enterprises, and all forms of organization appeal to you. You should direct, lead, build, write, and reform along the most advanced lines. Architects, sculptors, industrial designers fit in well here. If you don't understand your mastership, you will drop to a 4 cycle. You must learn to function in two worlds: the subjective and the objective. Under all circumstances, keep your balance, and remember, a 22 cycle has the capacity to tear down everything with the same efficiency it builds them up. In the negative aspect, there is the suggestion that you could very easily turn to the destructive side.

Alpha 21

THE BIRTH YEAR CYCLE

1 Birth Year Cycle — You prefer to keep moving all the time and you find it hard to restrain your boundless energy. Your mature desire is toward self-expression, which will help you to continue your life's work on an entirely different basis, so that you can gain personal recognition for past efforts. Since you often spend time alone, you should have some hobby or avocation that encourages your creative thinking and helps to create dialog with others.

2 Birth Year Cycle — You have harmony and protection waiting for you in your later years. If you retire, get yourself a hobby such as stamp or antique collecting. Do not allow yourself to remain idle because, when you do, you'll start feeling sorry for yourself and neglected. If you can enter some kind of local politics or work for a philanthropic group, you will enjoy serving in a capacity where your adaptability and conservative nature will be appreciated.

3 Birth Year Cycle — This is a time of life to enjoy your friends and hobbies. Always find a creative channel for your talents and mix with youthful people. Do not worry about time because, if you do, you will tend to become nervous and very critical in this cycle.

4 Birth Year Cycle — Since you may not be compelled to work for a living, you should find a hobby or avocation that will sustain you physically and emotionally. Health, nutrition and exercise are also important to you, and you need to spend sufficient time doing things with the groups in which you function, such as your family, your community, or local governments.

5 Birth Year Cycle — You will be free to do as you please and make any changes you wish. Travel and meet new and interesting people during this cycle. Always try to enter fully into the various phases of your activities. If you choose to retire, take pains to keep your mind and body alert. Start some type of hobby or work that will utilize your initiative and understanding. Keep yourself free to make your own decisions and don't let possessions burden you; stay free and flexible. You're one of those people who will die with your boots on because you refuse to give up.

6 Birth Year Cycle — It is vital for you to give some type of service to your community. Make the adjustments around you necessary to obtain a complete and harmonious environment. In these later years, you will be able to enjoy the companionships you have developed throughout life — a time for your comfort and ease.

7 Birth Year Cycle — In this cycle you'll have all the time you need to do all the things you've always wanted to do but never had time for. The cycle brings a time for study, especially along psychological and philosophical lines. You would enjoy a home in the country because of the calm and quiet of the countryside which gives you the sense of deep inner peace that is so necessary to your peace of mind.

8 Birth Year Cycle — Natives of this cycle very rarely retire, and when they do, they often remain active in civic affairs. Assume responsibilities in connection with group welfare or charities, etc. By this time of life you should be materially secure and you should not be overly concerned with money matters. This cycle will give you the opportunity to learn life's real values. It will teach you to equalize your material and spiritual qualities.

9 Birth Year Cycle — You are most likely to remain young because of your avid interest in life. You're always ahead of the times. In order to stay active, take an interest in group work and other impersonal activities. When you feel you have a message to.tell the world, write it down. Communication of ideas is your pleasure even if it never gets published. Beware, there's a turnover in personal relationships during this cycle which includes marriage and other close ties.

11 Birth Year Cycle — You should have less tension in this cycle. Be sure you have an outlet for your energies that will reduce sensitivity and any tendency to neurosis. You should take up some kind of group work, such as civic affairs or community politics. Think very little about accumulating worldly goods. Be most careful about attracting bad publicity.

22 Birth Year Cycle — The 22 Birth Year Cycle is the same as the 22 Birth Day Cycle. This is a highly-evolved period with great creative and/or great destructive potential, depending on how you express your special knowledge and insight.

Alpha 22

THE GOAL

1 Goal — You have independence of spirit. You will need to apply yourself to a single purpose or line of work. You should always use your inner resources to find new methods that are uniquely your own. You must never admit that you cannot attain your dreams. Be sure to concentrate on a definite outlet for your talents, and never let anyone change your commitment to what you believe is right. You will need to cooperate in all your personal relationships, but never let anyone else take your originality away from you.

2 Goal — Your sole purpose in life should be to develop understanding of others. You must absorb all the practical knowledge you can about life. Other people will come to you from time to time for your advice. You gain knowledge through experience, it is always your greatest teacher and what you have learned should be passed on to others. You will be very sensitive to others, but try to avoid going to extremes in this area. Do not become too personal in your interactions with those around you. You may need to build an emotional wall around yourself so you won't absorb too much of other people's personalities at the risk of your own.

3 Goal — As you go through life, you will learn how to give of yourself creatively. You will enjoy your work as long as it's of a creative nature. Always be sure to concentrate on meeting people who can contribute constructive ideas. It is very important for you to dress as attractively as your budget permits. Choose your colors tastefully. Always express your natural charm and stay optimistic about everything. You suffer from a lack of confidence at times. Don't let it create a false superiority complex. Arrogance will cause selfishness of the worst sort and will detract from your inherent good qualities.

4 Goal — Your life is built on your sense of organization. You have a need to serve, to produce, and also to be thorough and systematic. Develop your power of concentration and learn all you can about human values. You should have qualities of patience, loyalty, and endurance. There is a warning light in your life: your chief enemy is "worry." It will be the cause for most of your physical upsets. You can help to reduce your tendency to worry by hard work and exercise. You'll find that it is the best medicine for your bodily ills. Take special care with your health; give immediate attention to infection of any kind.

5 Goal — You're always going to have a lot of changes in your life. Learn to accept change easily, and enjoy many different types of life. You're going to meet many different people with many and different occupations. As you travel through life, you should free yourself from unnecessary obligations. Use your time constructively and always depend on your native intuition with all life's little problems. You like to travel and, by seeing and doing things, you learn things beyond mere formal education. Remember that "Fact is always more important than theory." You should exercise your ingenuity, and learn to discard as you go. Seek, investigate, and discover so that you can remain mentally alert and physically agile.

6 Goal — You need to be cheerful, efficient, and restrained in your behavior. You also feel a great need for balance in your personal relationships. Never run from those domestic problems that you always seem to find. Try to lend a helping hand to those who are less able than you are. You should do work for your community or your country; be in an advisory capacity when you can. When it comes to your family, serve them well, very well, and your rewards will always be great.

7 *Goal* — You should strive to understand the disturbances that offset your world. You have a gift for analysis; learn the value of your keen mental observations. Learn all you can about life to increase your store of knowledge. You should never be overly critical of others' behavior until you have learned to perfect your own behavior and spiritual qualities. You should learn the value of silence, and learn how to build the power within you. Opportunities in life tend to come to you instead of you trying to seek them out for yourself.

8 *Goal* — You will learn that there is nothing in life which is too big for you to try or, if you apply yourself, that you can't understand. Show the world the power within you; concentrate on attaining your rightful place in life. Learn the proper use of money; develop efficiency and management in all your affairs. Do not be tempted to express your demanding and aggressive attitude. Exercise discretion and self-control, and you will transmit the feeling to other people that you have "arrived." You know you can do this without officiousness or arrogance.

9 *Goal* — You should live your life without prejudice. Realize that there will always be flaws in human relationships, and learn the value of putting others before yourself. It's important to have personal ambitions, but don't let your ambitions overshadow the service you can render to others. Give love, sympathy, and understanding to all who seek your aid but do not become emotionally involved in their problems. Fulfill yourself and your life's obligations by developing your inner resources to their greatest potential.

11 *Goal* — You must specialize. You should elevate everything you think and do to a plane of pure inspiration. Stimulate your mind with new discoveries, new principles, and new inventions. Offer your talents to the world. Always trust in your own intuition and depend upon your divine sources for guidance. Do not try to monopolize center stage; leave something for others, to help them find themselves. Stay away from people who will try to drain your highly-charged

energies. You may need to build a wall around yourself to restrain people who would try to profit by your talents and appropriate your personality for their own benefit.

22 Goal — You are guided by a pure master number. There is no number higher than 22. Because of this, you must learn to serve humanity in the largest and most constructive way. Your work is to uplift other people, to improve them, and to help reform the standards of the world in which you live. You may work in some connection with the government, or enter some field which is connected with affairs of international scope. You have executive capacity — productive and managerial at the same time. Do not lose sight of your spiritual obligations. Always be practical and inspired in equal amounts.

Alpha 23

THE ACHIEVEMENT

1 Achievement — You need to be direct because there is going to be a lot of activity around you. This is a time for you to develop leadership. At different times you're going to be standing alone and there will be new responsibilities that may be added to those you already have.

2 Achievement — You must motivate yourself through cooperation. You need to acquire poise, tact, and consideration for others. Learn how not to be selfish when you're acquiring possessions or money; selfishness will darken your outlook on life. You're a sensitive person, and you should not let your sensitivity become a problem around other people. If you do, it will boomerang back toward you. You will have a deep and lasting affection for your parents.

3 Achievement — It is very important for you to nurture your friendships and to learn sincere respect for others. Be sure to use your time properly so that you understand yourself inside and out. Your critical thoughts should be kept to yourself. Use knowledge and reason to enhance your imagination and it will add luster to your talents. There will be many opportunities you cannot afford to miss; be prepared. You will have an active love life, but take caution not to break hearts just for the pleasure you find in it. Do not consume other people's valuable time. Establish harmony in the home, shop, or office. Keep all your appointments and be on time.

4 Achievement — Your lifestyle may move along at a slow pace, but it will build well and securely for your future. This is a period of growth, a time that will require a lot of self-control and effort and service to others. You must manage all departments of your life properly in order to have a strong foundation for your future. Try to keep normal hours, and try to conserve all the vitality you can. No matter what project you may begin, always stay with it until the project is completed.

5 Achievement — There will be many new experiences for you. These new experiences will come to you unexpected and surprisingly. Contacting other people and traveling will play a major role in your life. Your home or love life may not be quiet and settled, but a lot of life's little problems will disappear, depending on your ability to adapt to life's ups and downs. When you do business with others, do not speculate; avoid all out and out gambles.

6 Achievement — You are not to be selfish with others. Learn to help yourself by helping other people. This does not mean complete self-sacrifice. If you're not already married, then you probably will be. You should work with large groups or possibly take responsibility in some group doing work for the government. Service to other people will play a very important part in your life.

7 Achievement — Look into yourself, find out who you really are. Examine all of your motives and desires. You will enjoy working in occupations requiring mental and technical skills, such as the behind-the-scenes jobs in radio, the movies, research, etc. You're protected financially; but how large the return may be is up to you.

8 Achievement — It is time for you to assume your rightful place in life. Cultivate your ideas; learn balance and judgment. You'll have power for authority and recognition. Watch out that you don't push too hard; you'll lose both your reputation and finances. There will be trouble in your world unless you control your prejudice and your desire to dominate. If you don't learn to control these emotions, you will risk losing the things you love, not to mention the mental anguish it will cause you. Take hold of your emotions and strive for balance in all your relationships. Always deal with people in authority; supervise, organize, and produce whenever you can.

9 Achievement — You must learn understanding without losing your idealism. When you try to hold onto things by force, you will lose a lot — possibly even the very thing you wish most to retain. This is a successful time of life for you. Your success will come from your creative mind. There are still a lot of frustrations in your life brought on by your own anxieties. People do depend on you, so find an impersonal way to release your emotions. Cooperate and enjoy.

11 Achievement — This is a time in life that may be difficult for you to handle. You will experience some deep spiritual happenings; you will find these happenings hard to express to others. You will have problems with partnerships unless you learn the value of cooperation and consideration for others. You will be involved in publicity of one kind or another. You may experience some unusual occurrences of an unpredictable nature. Life brings prominence, so be poised and relaxed under any and all circumstances.

22 Achievement — Watch out that you don't suffer as a result of your trying to take on projects that are too large or too difficult for you to handle. Because of your broad vision, you may take on far too much responsibility, and fail as a result. This is a good time to expand your interests, but be careful how you expand yourself. Do it consciously and with a plan. If you wish to succeed in business, try international affairs where you'll do well.

Alpha 24

THE DEMAND

1 Demand — You must have will power. Take your stand and don't succumb to the temptation to run away from the things you'd prefer not to face. Be willing to admit when you are wrong, but do not show a lack of ability to make up your mind. Learn to stand by your first decisions.

2 Demand — Try not to go to extremes over minor matters. Don't let other people take advantage of your softness. You are often too moody and too possessive. Learn to be less selfish. Don't worry or be afraid of making a mistake. Don't be worried about someone hurting you; face life realistically and with an open mind.

3 Demand — You should make the most of your abilities. You should avoid the appearance of being so anti-social and so overly critical of others. Learn to show your other side: your charm, good manners and pleasant appearance. Use your good diction and vocabulary. Be sure to criticize your own work and outlook before you blast at other people.

4 Demand — You have a tendency to be too formal and too intolerant around other people. Learn to appreciate other people's outlook and quit going to extremes in your insistence upon order and tradition. You worry needlessly about the small matters of everyday life. Your concern that you're always overworked may just be an indication that you're exceptionally lazy.

5 Demand — Your habit of trying anything once could get you into trouble. Try to learn not to indulge in change just for the sake of change. If you persist, you'll fail to learn the practical experience of life. Think about the reasons behind your variable actions and your desire for constant change. Do not let your curiosity get the better of you. Since you have a desire for knowledge, learn through real research and investigations instead of aimless seeking. Be careful about experimenting too freely in sexual matters. You must find a niche in life and develop it — love, life, career. These are the answers.

6 Demand — You tend to think your ideas and values are the best, which will eventually lead to some bitter disappointments for you. You do have good judgment, but learn to judge your own ideas and standards before you offer them to others. You're going to have problems with marriage, or with dating others, because you like to be the leader. When you find out that you cannot always be the leader, you may want to break off all ties. Learn not to be so smug and opinionated. If you can learn to meet others more than halfway, and be willing sometimes to sit on the sidelines without offering so much advice, then you'll go through this time of life with no problems.

7 Demand — You're a very difficult person, either overly proud, suffering from a superiority complex, or completely the other way, too sensitive and self-effacing. You insist upon escaping from life because sometimes you don't want to face the realities. You will enter deep moods and allow despondency to grow within you because life seems harsh and unfair. You will gain peace by having faith in yourself and by putting your faith in the hands of the divine force: it's good therapy.

8 Demand — Sometimes your drive for power is too great for your own good. Money represents power in your often materialistic world. You shouldn't place so much emphasis on money. Be careful that your desire for material wealth doesn't affect your physical body and limit you completely. Try to develop a constructive outlook and avoid mental strain under all circumstances, and strive to achieve a good, balanced approach to life.

Alpha 25

THE ATMOSPHERE

1 Atmosphere — A, J, S — When it comes to the goal you are trying to attain, it is important to learn the power of concentration. To reach your own goals and to take advantage of any leadership opportunities that become open to you, you will need discipline and dedication.

2 Atmosphere — B, T — In this time of life, it is important to gather all the information you can about yourself and your future. Open yourself up to experiences that will supply you with inner knowledge: possessions that will last for a long time to come. You must learn all you can about every phase of your life.

3 Atmosphere — C, L, U — Concentrate on the work that appeals most to you. This will help to keep your physical energies intact. You must go out of your way to meet people, find the people who can help and assist you in your needs. Don't permit yourself to scatter your forces just so you can break up the routine of your life.

4 Atmosphere — D, M — Do not make any radical changes at this time of your life. You must stay organized in all departments of your life. You must keep up your vitality, and at the same time, you should develop yourself mentally, physically, and spiritually for the future.

5 Atmosphere — E, N, W — You will experience some unexpected events in your life at this time. You need a certain amount of freedom, if you're tied down by the circumstances around you, you will rebel. This is a good time to become an opportunist, but you must move quickly. Remember that you can never depend on complete stability or set rules during this part of your life.

6 Atmosphere — F, O, X — You'll find that there will be a lot of adjustments for you right now — changes of one kind or another. Be careful not to revolt or lose sight of the important things around you. Try to create harmony in all your associations with other people.

7 Atmosphere — G, P, Y — You're going to be very outgoing and successful as soon as you learn to organize and discipline your thoughts. You need to study some new techniques for self-improvement — to broaden your horizons.

8 Atmosphere — H, Q, Z — This is the time of life for you to reevaluate your opportunities. You must learn to undertake without grumbling the duties that may be assigned to you. To assure a strong foundation for what you wish to accomplish, you must evaluate everything from the ground up. Always be willing to accept authority. If you want to be a complete failure, just keep using those high-handed methods to get what you want.

9 Atmosphere — I, R — You are going to meet with many different experiences that should add to your store of knowledge and understanding. Travel should be a part of your life. There will be a lot of changes around you and some terminations will occur. Refuse to let life tear at your emotions. Learn to live life with ease, otherwise your physical well-being will suffer.

11 Atmosphere — K — This is an excellent time in your life for inventing things. This is your creative time, a time for teaching, writing and lecturing. It is a time that inspires you with new incentives. Stay balanced, avoid moods, and be careful of going off on tangents that have little relation to the more basic things in your life.

22 Atmosphere — V — Learn to extend your interests in life to a wider audience. You have the power to develop your talents, to increase your knowledge and understanding, but learn to control your temper and aggressiveness.

Alpha 26

THE PASSAGE

1 Passage — *A* — There is going to be a change either physically or mentally and most likely you'll be making a change of address or employment position. When you're trying a new idea or starting a new enterprise, it is especially necessary to follow through with it. Protect your head, all parts of the head should be given care.

J — Your mind is always fluctuating when you're trying to find which way is right. When you are undecided about things, ask a more experienced person for advice before you start making important moves. This is a time in your life to capitalize on all opportunities.

S — You are going to see all your hidden problems; your whole life up to now is going to surface in front of your eyes. You may experience some unwanted emotional problems and you may have to tear down your entire lifestyle. During all of this, you will be an individual who is able to make a fresh start for the future, for advantages further up the road of life. You can avoid greater problems if you will learn to control your fluctuating emotions and use reason to determine the right course of action to take.

2 Passage — *B* — There will be a lot of unusual circumstances in your life. There will be physical ills unless you keep up your health and hygiene. You will find you change in moods a lot, with a tendency to go into deep depression. For peace of mind, try marriage, or try working harder at the marriage you already have.

T — You'll find this is a good time for marriage. A solid partnership will help you with all of the added responsibilities that are coming your way. It's a very good time to build your resources.

3 Passage C — You have good insight into life, but you sometimes go completely out of bounds in your desire to fulfill yourself. Be careful of indulging your ego, and concentrate on doing your most constructive type of work.

L — You must concentrate on one task at a time if you are to have complete mental balance. This is very necessary for you when you're trying to make any clear-cut decisions about life. Don't get into any emotional conflicts — it will only lead to accidents. You will find travel is possible now and it's a wonderful emotional outlet.

U — You wish to destroy things around you that have hurt you in the past, and you probably will. Watch your emotional indulgence because you have a tendency to indulge your ego-centeredness. You try too hard to attract attention. You can change this attitude and relieve your anxiety by learning to give and take without emotionalism. For an emotional outlet, try writing or acting.

4 Passage — D — You may find pressure put upon you through your business or profession. There is going to be an offer of travel in connection with your career and you may find a promotion or a new position of authority because of work that you have done well. Stay with the traditional ways of life and don't overwork yourself. Too much pressure will cause you a lot of physical difficulties.

M — You are going to have trouble with others because of your chief problem: neglecting people and things around you. When it comes to your personal problems, you let them get so close to you that you can't see how to solve them. You must learn to accept your responsibilities and to care about other people.

5 Passage — E — There is going to be a lot of activity around you. You're going to have new opportunities and a lot of travel. Because of your broad outlook on life, you will be especially attractive to the opposite sex. There may be a love affair which will absorb you to the point that you will lose a lot by letting it take up most of your valuable time. When you finally decide on an acceptable way of life, don't let anyone detract you from your course.

N — You will defy the way things are supposed to be done in the world and you will have to pay too high a price for having done so. Because you are ambitious for worldly goods, financial gain is usually attained in this time of life. Be careful not to deplete your physical resources through abuse of your body.

W — There will be a lot of hectic changes around you. Because of your strong desire for activity, you may exhaust your energy supply, which could result in some very poor timing in highly speculative ventures.

6 Passage — *F* — You are secure enough materially that now you can enjoy giving service to both family and community. You should accept new responsibilities, such as marriage, children, etc. Be careful, however, not to take on more responsibilities than necessary. Try some creative type of work; it is an excellent time for it. Remember, when you are inclined to magnify an unpleasant situation around you, look for the bright side; you're just thinking negatively again.

O — There will be an accumulation of material things. If you're not already married, then this is a good time for it. Married or not, you may cause yourself some problems by living with relatives or trying to raise children of a former marriage. Because you are more emotional at this time of life than other people, you should learn how to depersonalize your feelings.

X — During this time of life, you will find it hard to break free of the problems that have surrounded you. Because of your complex emotions, you'll most likely create situations for which no one ever bargained. Be sure to pay attention to your health. Strong emotions may take their toll on your heart.

7 Passage — *G* — You have a desire for material gain, so why not give yourself an incentive to improve the circumstances around you. Use good judgment and improve your finances gradually; in the attempt to improve them too fast you could lose everything. This is an excellent time for perfecting an invention or writing a book.

P — You tend to dwell in self-indulgence and self-delusion. Setting around thinking what to do is going to retard your progress. Watch out for the people with whom you associate. They may be the wrong type of people; be wary of deceit. Be sure to undertake all legal and financial matters with caution.

Y — Life confuses your aims, but this is a good time for study or research and a good time to build your life's structure slowly. You should give to others what you have already tried and tested. When you find difficulties in your personal relationships, or especially in marriage, analyze your own role first. You're a person who has an aloof quality about yourself.

8 Passage — *H* — This is a time for financial gain — if you adhere to what you have already learned throughout your life so far. You will do well if you don't let your emotions sidetrack you. There is a good opportunity for you to raise capital or to put your business on a sound footing — a chance to acquire the type of authority for which you have prepared yourself. For those people who are able to fulfill themselves through their offspring, invest some time with your children — or make plans which involve children.

Q — There is a tendency toward material gain by slow and sound methods which may bring prestige in unexpected and unusual ways. Your life's structure has many protective aspects. There are great benefits through family and marriage connections. Learn to value your intuitive faculties and put them to practical use, especially in business and professional matters. Do not overlook the benevolent side of your character. Develop an inner strength for your outside responsibilities.

Z — It's very important for you to prepare a proper base of action to reach the heights that you wish to attain in life. Learn to employ the authority you have attained wisely. Be self-sufficient without being coldly detached. Remember there are certain dangers involved if you are too concerned with material progress.

9 Passage — *I* — Your lifestyle shows possible improvement through travel or public work. You must not be too self-centered or too self-aggrandizing. Your health could be affected by the intensity of your emotions. You should find some creative outlet for your talents.

R — You have a broad outlook on life and you tend to take life in a suitably depersonalized way. You must not think negatively because that will cause difficulties for you. Always try and think positively. Control your emotions so you don't cause yourself accidents when you are in the grip of your anxieties.

11 Passage — *K* — Life around you may seem unusual at times. You're a highly inspired person, but you may be too visionary for your own good. You must keep your nervous tension to a minimum and watch your self-indulgence.

22 Passage — *V* — Life may cause you to reach beyond your normal limits. You will have a drive for acclaim and a desire to reach exceptional heights in your own special sphere. As you go through life, you will stumble often before you climb to the top. Obstacles are many, but the effort and persistence will bear fruit. There will be travel to great distances and wide-scale or international contacts. Remember, when you become extravagant with finances and emotions, you lose control of your most vital resources.

Alpha 28

THE ESSENCE

1 Essence — Concentrate on your goals. Disciplined effort is vital to your well-being. Always conserve energy and be especially careful with the condition of your body and nervous system. Be ambitious, inventive, and progressive.

2 Essence — You are to stop, look, and listen. Learn to study your ideas, to move slowly, and to use tact. Strive for peaceful surroundings because very soon life is going to bring you some stimulating events and/or disruptive conditions (depending on your development and your ability to depersonalize your outlook).

3 Essence — You need to learn to live in the world outside yourself. Forget about your personal doubts and worries and meet some new faces. You may meet someone of importance. Social activities will help to lighten some of life's problems and it will give you a more optimistic view. Because you're not happy with yourself at times, you're going to have a problem with all your personal relationships over the most trifling problems. When you learn to get out of yourself and take an interest in other people, you will be able to forget your little personal problems and experience real peace and satisfaction.

4 Essence — You have a good foundation going for you in life at this time. You're going to find out that work is very necessary to control your tension. You have a physical and emotional need for security. Marriage or a strong personal relationship will help this feeling. You must keep those little personal problems of life away from you; if not, those problems will dominate your entire sphere of influence.

5 Essence — You may wish to change from the standard "9 to 5" routine of the world and try some unusual and up-to-the-minute ideas. Go out and meet new friends and try to free yourself from some of your minor and unimportant duties. But keep an open mind and be careful of hasty judgments. Don't waste your energy on the nagging problems that are so unrelated to your long-range goals.

6 Essence — There will always be some personality problems that will require diplomatic handling, but you must not become involved in small issues. Learn to look at your life more objectively. Give your body the proper care it needs because the responsibilities that you're going to assume will put a staggering load on your body.

7 Essence — This is a very good time in your life to enter work in the field of movies, radio, television, law, religion, and all types of research. It is advisable to move slowly and try to be less concerned with the material things of life and more concerned with the mental and spiritual development of your life. To help your health and emotional well-being, try spending some time in the country. Keep your diet and blood pressure under control.

8 Essence — You want to be in a position of authority wherever you are. It is very important for you to keep active and to contact those who contribute information that will help to promote your personal progress. Be careful of over working, control your finances wisely, and avoid too much muscular strain. You need to develop a system of relaxation to avoid future health problems.

9 Essence — You should spend a good amount of time traveling. Now is a good time to work with large groups or to work in creative enterprises. There will be some terminations and conclusions for you when you're thinking negatively. Fulfillment comes to you only when you're thinking constructively. Learn to get rid of anything that's blocking your progress. Avoid too many emotional pulls, and learn to project yourself outward.

11 Essence — This is a wonderful time in your life to develop your talents, your inventiveness, and it is also a good time for possible publicity. It's a time for stimulating events as well as hectic conditions, depending on your own development and your ability to retain your balance.

22 Essence — Your physical difficulties can be overcome by hard work. This will also help to make your life more secure. You are going to take some risks to broaden your interests, but do not branch out too widely or take on so many responsibilities that you cannot give each of them your full personal attention. You work well with syndicates, chain stores, international problems. Be realistic and humble in your personal dealings.

Alpha 29

THE AGE

1 Age — The age one covers ages: 9-10 yrs., 18-19 yrs., 27-28 yrs., 36-37 yrs., 45-46 yrs., 54-55 yrs., 63-64 yrs., 72-73 yrs., etc.

This is a time for the completion of old projects and the beginning of new ones. Everything no longer essential to your life should be cleared away before you make a new start.

2 Age — The age two covers ages: 5-6 yrs., 14-15 yrs., 23-24 yrs., 32-33 yrs., 41-42 yrs., 50-51 yrs., 59-60 yrs., 68-69 yrs., 77-78 yrs., etc.

There may be some disruption and excitement in your life at this time. There is need for you to have patience and pay attention to the details which are extremely important. Cooperation is paramount. Contacts are necessary, and some adjustments (especially at home) may be needed. Because of a certain amount of tension, develop a smooth-running plan of action.

3 Age — The age three covers ages: 1-2 yrs., 10-20 yrs., 19-20 yrs., 37-38 yrs., 46-47 yrs., 55-56 yrs., 64-65 yrs., 73-74 yrs., etc.

There is an indication of originality and creativity and a new beginning in relation to the personal year connected with this period. You should learn to soften your aggressiveness. You also need to lower your tension and initiate a step-by-step program to improve your communications with other people.

4 Age — The age four covers ages: 6-7 yrs., 15-16 yrs., 24-25 yrs., 33-34 yrs., 42-43 yrs., 51-52 yrs., 60-61 yrs., 69-70 yrs., etc.

Influences around you may be confining to the point that you will rebel or stubbornly resist the circumstances that may arise. You may wish to withdraw within yourself and completely forget your obligations to be cooperative. This is a time for completion. You're going to find your relationships in love and marriage threatened because you're always blasting at someone and tearing down your own foundations. You should take greater interest in your work and your health.

5 Age — The age five covers ages: 2-3 yrs., 11-12 yrs., 20-21 yrs., 29-30 yrs., 38-39 yrs., 47-48 yrs., 56-57 yrs., 65-66 yrs., 74-75 yrs., etc.

You change things around you too hastily. You should learn to be more cautious and more attentive to detail. Watch your moods because fluctuations will affect your major decisions. You're often self-indulgent and rash, especially when you don't get your own way. You may feel the right way to express yourself is through sensual gratification; be careful. There may be a change of home or career or position; if so, you may also gain a new attitude about yourself and your responsibilities.

6 Age — The age six covers ages: 7-8 yrs., 16-17 yrs., 25-26 yrs., 34-35 yrs., 43-44 yrs., 52-53 yrs., 61-62 yrs., 70-71 yrs., etc.

Adjustments in your life are in order. You must learn to use the power you have within you. This will be done when you can feel that everything you touch is in order and your mind is attuned to its own inner strengths. Your finances should be improved during this building time. There may be some family problems, especially regarding money matters. Perhaps a new home may be established to create more harmony in your family affairs. Always look deep within yourself, be organized, help others.

7 Age — The age seven covers ages: 3-4 yrs., 12-13 yrs., 21-22 yrs., 30-31 yrs., 39-40 yrs., 48-49 yrs., 57-58 yrs., 66-67 yrs., 75-76 yrs., etc.

Whatever you decide to do with your life will require extensive research and study. There is a side of you that scatters and disrupts everything, so be sure to take more than average care with work done with papers, writing, or speech, etc. If this is done right, your self-expression should take a constructive turn. Your personality also has another side that insists upon conventional values so that you are able to guide things to acceptable and predictable results. Don't be surprised if what you start now doesn't come to fruition until after your next birthday.

8 Age — The age eight covers ages: 8-9 yrs., 17-18 yrs., 26-27 yrs., 35-36 yrs., 44-45 yrs., 53-54 yrs., 62-63 yrs., 71-72 yrs., etc.

Business matters are doubly influenced but you are pushing too hard, and your attempt to dominate the situations that arise creates problems. If you are in a managerial position, be fully aware that as you move to the top your authority demands more of you and that you owe more to those who serve you in a subordinate capacity. Always be willing to let go of what is not necessary for your progress. Financial loss will occur if your foundations are insecure and if you persist in believing that money is the only source of advancement. Don't allow your emotions to detract you from clear thinking.

9 Age — The age nine covers ages: 4-5 yrs., 13-14 yrs., 22-23 yrs., 31-32 yrs., 40-41 yrs., 49-50 yrs., 58-59 yrs., 67-68 yrs., 76-77 yrs., etc.

If you are doing any public work, this is the right time for it. Life presents opportunities to capitalize on your talents. To gain fulfillment from your past efforts, you must be more tolerant of those with whom you work and live. Because your emotions lie very near the surface, circumstances may take their toll on your health. Do not display your emotions carelessly. Since your opinions tend to be fixed, be sure you're able to back them up with facts if you wish for constructive results. There will be some travel in connection with your work. Consider all changes carefully and once you have laid your plans, revise your affairs accordingly. Also, consider all the people who might be affected by your decisions.

Alpha 31

THE PERSONAL YEAR

1 Personal Year — Energy — You are to push outward, forcefully, dynamically, and ceaselessly toward your goals. Your natural good health will give you vitality; your mind will give you determination, and your spirit will provide forcefulness. This is a time for starting new things: life, love, work, study and creative endeavors. You're a pioneer. What you do in this cycle of life will be with you for at least nine more years, and sometimes a lifetime. Use your time wisely.

2 Personal Year — Sensitivity — This is the time to learn the difference between the positive and the negative poles of life. Your spirit is going to divide itself so you are able to learn cooperation. You will learn to assert yourself, to see life from all sides, to resolve differences diplomatically, to gather unto yourself, to control your moods, to be receptive, agreeable, sentimental, balanced, imaginative, and sensitive. During this period, you will cling to what you wish to retain from the past.

3 Personal Year — Expression — You are going to learn the meaning of creative expression. You'll be able to put your ideas across to other people much more easily. Your soul will touch your emotions so that your conscience will spring into action. This period frees the critical side of you. This is a time to cultivate your creative talents, and you should express yourself easily through your well rounded personality.

4 Personal Year — Foundation — You are going to learn to build your life from the four major principles: the spirit, the soul, the mind, and the body. You are beginning to learn your fundamental lessons and how to meet your limitations. Unless your body functions satisfactorily, you cannot work well with the other principles — soul, spirit, and mind. You're going to learn to systematize and organize your life. You should build inner as well as outer security. You will attain your greatest benefits from work that deals with form.

5 Personal Year — Freedom — In the last four years, you have learned to work with your personal limitations. Now you'll have to look outside yourself to discover what lies beyond your inner resources. You will need to learn how to use your outer senses, the five fingers and their sensitive tips, the five toes which give you a sense of balance and direction, and the five extensions of the body: the arms, the legs, and the head. With these, you are able to express yourself through freedom of action. You'll have a strong desire to be different and to be free of encumbrances. You're going to be physically active and seek new experiences.

6 Personal Year — Adjustment — You're going to want to work closely with your family or your community. You'll enjoy extending a helping hand to others and showing them how they can adjust to their circumstances. You should be aware of all the necessary duties that are part of any group problem, including those close at hand as well as those involving business, professional, or community problems. Your feelings and practical values are of equal importance now. Because of your innate understanding, you are able to help other people in a practical way.

7 Personal Year — Perfection — You will be making efforts to work constructively, and with a desire to reach outside yourself for perfection. You have taken six steps of your life in the past six years to learn inner and outer development. You are now ready to examine yourself and your motives in order to improve every possible aspect of your life. You will need to withdraw from material advancement and to analyze every move you make. Take action without aggression. You are in an area of your life which is called "the year of completion." Because you are in a 7 year, you're in good hands: the number 7 has mystical and religious attributes. The number 7 also encompasses our week, our color spectrum, and the notes in the musical scale. You will learn to wait for things to come to you instead of forcing issues too energetically. You are able to see things clearly, but you may not always be able to define quite so clearly what you have seen or felt.

8 Personal Year — Organization — In the past you have gone through a period of self-analysis, and now you're ready to project your new-found energy toward the world. You are concerned with demonstrating your abilities and with building your inner power in constructive ways. It is important to learn how to recognize and utilize your resources, and with twice the qualification you will then be ready to do things on a larger scale. Because you are concerned with form and matter, you may tend to overlook matters of spiritual significance. Learn crystallization and organization.

9 Personal Year — Understanding — You have completed a full nine year cycle and are now ready to do something for the world at large. In this phase, you are associated with all public matters, humanitarian affairs, and global issues. You will reap your greatest harvest through objectivity and through compassion for everyone, great and small. Look at life from every angle, not just the heart. A 9 Personal Year is a boundless circle without beginning or end. This is your "year of fulfillment," but to gain its benefits you must understand the cyclical nature of being and recognize that what you throw out often comes right back to you. People who become self-centered, demanding and possessive will fail to profit by the opportunities which surround them during this year. Negative thinking will rob you of the rewards life has to offer and will destroy the joys of your accomplishments. Therefore, concentrate on the positive and learn from the principles of life you are able to detect from the lessons you have learned along the way.

THE ALPHASCAN 2000 WORKSHEETS

A	B	C	D	E	F	G	H	I		1st, Degree
1	2	3	4	5	6	7	8	9		
J	K	L	M	N	O	P	Q	R		2nd, Degree
10	11	12	13	14	15	16	17	18		
S	T	U	V	W	X	Y	Z			3rd, Degree
19	20	21	22	23	24	25	26			

A	B	C	D	E	F	G	H	I		1st, Degree
1	2	3	4	5	6	7	8	9		
J	K	L	M	N	O	P	Q	R		2nd, Degree
S	T	U	V	W	X	Y	Z			3rd, Degree
1	2	3	4	5	6	7	8			

Each letter in the English alphabet has a corresponding numerical value which, as described in the introduction, have been developed over centuries of experimentation to match up with certain emotional and physical qualities. In developing your own Alphascan 2000 chart, it will be helpful to memorize the letter and number values. But for quick reference, you may refer to the chart above. In the spaces provided on these pages, you may write the name of any person you are charting and the appropriate numbers for each characteristic. At that point, you can go back to the Answer section and discover what the numbers tell you about them.

THE DESIRE denotes drive and ambition directed toward specific goals. The Desire is your point of view. Add only the vowels in the First, Middle, and Last name.

NAMES   NUMBERS

_____   _____

_____   _____

_____   _____

THE RESOURCE is the framework of your Desire. It provides a background for the Desire and shows you how to fulfill your Expression. Add only the Consonants of the First, Middle, and Last name.

NAMES   NUMBERS

_____   _____

_____   _____

_____   _____

THE EXPRESSION is the side of you which is most visible to the world around you. It suggests your talents, your behavior, and your visible approach to life, whether you have changed your name, added a nickname, taken on a married name, or not. The Birth Name, which is the basis of the Expression, stays with you for life. Add all letters in your Full Name.

NAMES   NUMBERS

_____   _____

_____   _____

_____   _____

THE FOUNDATION shapes your outlook on life and may promote or retard your progress. It affects your mental and physical approach. It is determined by the first letter of the First Name only.

A	B	C	D	E	F	G	H	I	1st, Degree
1	2	3	4	5	6	7	8	9	
J	K	L	M	N	O	P	Q	R	2nd, Degree
10	11	12	13	14	15	16	17	18	
S	T	U	V	W	X	Y	Z		3rd, Degree
19	20	21	22	23	24	25	26		

A	B	C	D	E	F	G	H	I	1st, Degree
1	2	3	4	5	6	7	8	9	
J	K	L	M	N	O	P	Q	R	2nd, Degree
S	T	U	V	W	X	Y	Z		3rd, Degree
1	2	3	4	5	6	7	8		

THE KEY OF LIFE is the clue that indicates how you can expand your potential, especially in relation to your vocation. Add all numbers of the First Name only.

A	B	C	D	E	F	G	H	I		1st, Degree
1	2	3	4	5	6	7	8	9		
J	K	L	M	N	O	P	Q	R		2nd, Degree
10	11	12	13	14	15	16	17	18		
S	T	U	V	W	X	Y	Z			3rd, Degree
19	20	21	22	23	24	25	26			

A	B	C	D	E	F	G	H	I		1st, Degree
1	2	3	4	5	6	7	8	9		
J	K	L	M	N	O	P	Q	R		2nd, Degree
S	T	U	V	W	X	Y	Z			3rd, Degree
1	2	3	4	5	6	7	8			

NAMES　　　　　　　　　　NUMBERS

—————————　　　—————————

—————————　　　—————————

—————————　　　—————————

THE FIRST VOWEL is an indication of the individual's emotional and spiritual depth. It is determined by the first Vowel of the First Name only. (Note: if the first vowel is a Y, as in the name Lynda, its value will be a 9, not 7.)

A	B	C	D	E	F	G	H	I	1st, Degree
1	2	3	4	5	6	7	8	9	
J	K	L	M	N	O	P	Q	R	2nd, Degree
10	11	12	13	14	15	16	17	18	
S	T	U	V	W	X	Y	Z		3rd, Degree
19	20	21	22	23	24	25	26		

A	B	C	D	E	F	G	H	I	1st, Degree
1	2	3	4	5	6	7	8	9	
J	K	L	M	N	O	P	Q	R	2nd, Degree
S	T	U	V	W	X	Y	Z		3rd, Degree
1	2	3	4	5	6	7	8		

NAMES

NUMBERS

_____   _____

_____   _____

_____   _____

THE MISSING NUMBERS provide comparisons of the strengths and weaknesses of personality and emotion in the Birth Name. When you have determined all the number values of the letters in the full Birth Name, make a list of all missing numbers.

A	B	C	D	E	F	G	H	I		1st, Degree
1	2	3	4	5	6	7	8	9		
J	K	L	M	N	O	P	Q	R		2nd, Degree
10	11	12	13	14	15	16	17	18		
S	T	U	V	W	X	Y	Z			3rd, Degree
19	20	21	22	23	24	25	26			

A	B	C	D	E	F	G	H	I		1st, Degree
1	2	3	4	5	6	7	8	9		
J	K	L	M	N	O	P	Q	R		2nd, Degree
S	T	U	V	W	X	Y	Z			3rd, Degree
1	2	3	4	5	6	7	8			

NAMES   NUMBERS

_____   _____

_____   _____

_____   _____

THE ABUNDANCE is determined by the one or more numbers which appear more often than the others. It can suggest your greatest strength or your greatest weakness. Find the numbers which appear most frequently in the Full Name.

A	B	C	D	E	F	G	H	I	1st, Degree
1	2	3	4	5	6	7	8	9	
J	K	L	M	N	O	P	Q	R	2nd, Degree
10	11	12	13	14	15	16	17	18	
S	T	U	V	W	X	Y	Z		3rd, Degree
19	20	21	22	23	24	25	26		

A	B	C	D	E	F	G	H	I	1st, Degree
1	2	3	4	5	6	7	8	9	
J	K	L	M	N	O	P	Q	R	2nd, Degree
S	T	U	V	W	X	Y	Z		3rd, Degree
1	2	3	4	5	6	7	8		

NAMES

NUMBERS

_____   _____

_____   _____

_____   _____

THE SUBCONSCIOUS indicates your potential reactions under stress when you put down your learned defenses; this is the side of you the world seldom sees. Subtract the total number of the letters missing from your name from 9.

A	B	C	D	E	F	G	H	I	1st, Degree
1	2	3	4	5	6	7	8	9	
J	K	L	M	N	O	P	Q	R	2nd, Degree
10	11	12	13	14	15	16	17	18	
S	T	U	V	W	X	Y	Z		3rd, Degree
19	20	21	22	23	24	25	26		
A	B	C	D	E	F	G	H	I	1st, Degree
1	2	3	4	5	6	7	8	9	
J	K	L	M	N	O	P	Q	R	2nd, Degree
S	T	U	V	W	X	Y	Z		3rd, Degree
1	2	3	4	5	6	7	8		

NAMES   NUMBERS

_____   _____

_____   _____

_____   _____

THE FOUNDATION OF EXPRESSION is a key element in determining your chief traits, personal characteristics, and vocational possibilities. Total the numbers in the Full Name. How many letters are in the name?

A	B	C	D	E	F	G	H	I	1st, Degree
1	2	3	4	5	6	7	8	9	
J	K	L	M	N	O	P	Q	R	2nd, Degree
10	11	12	13	14	15	16	17	18	
S	T	U	V	W	X	Y	Z		3rd, Degree
19	20	21	22	23	24	25	26		

A	B	C	D	E	F	G	H	I	1st, Degree
1	2	3	4	5	6	7	8	9	
J	K	L	M	N	O	P	Q	R	2nd, Degree
S	T	U	V	W	X	Y	Z		3rd, Degree
1	2	3	4	5	6	7	8		

NAMES

_____

_____

_____

NUMBERS

_____

_____

_____

THE FIRST CYCLE is the period in which you learn your most fundamental lessons. This is the period when you are conditioned by home and education. It is the number of the Birth Month.

A	B	C	D	E	F	G	H	I	1st, Degree
1	2	3	4	5	6	7	8	9	
J	K	L	M	N	O	P	Q	R	2nd, Degree
10	11	12	13	14	15	16	17	18	
S	T	U	V	W	X	Y	Z		3rd, Degree
19	20	21	22	23	24	25	26		

A	B	C	D	E	F	G	H	I	1st, Degree
1	2	3	4	5	6	7	8	9	
J	K	L	M	N	O	P	Q	R	2nd, Degree
S	T	U	V	W	X	Y	Z		3rd, Degree
1	2	3	4	5	6	7	8		

NAMES   NUMBERS

_____   _____

_____   _____

_____   _____

THE SECOND CYCLE is the period when you establish yourself in the outside world. This is the period when you are conditioned by work, marriage, friendships, or other contacts. It is the number of the Birth Day.

A	B	C	D	E	F	G	H	I		1st, Degree
1	2	3	4	5	6	7	8	9		
J	K	L	M	N	O	P	Q	R		2nd, Degree
10	11	12	13	14	15	16	17	18		
S	T	U	V	W	X	Y	Z			3rd, Degree
19	20	21	22	23	24	25	26			
A	B	C	D	E	F	G	H	I		1st, Degree
1	2	3	4	5	6	7	8	9		
J	K	L	M	N	O	P	Q	R		2nd, Degree
S	T	U	V	W	X	Y	Z			3rd, Degree
1	2	3	4	5	6	7	8			

NAMES

NUMBERS

_____   _____

_____   _____

_____   _____

THE THIRD CYCLE is the period when you realign your life in keeping with your mature goals and self-satisfaction. This is the period when outside circumstances no longer upset your balance. It is the number of the Birth Year.

A	B	C	D	E	F	G	H	I		1st, Degree
1	2	3	4	5	6	7	8	9		
J	K	L	M	N	O	P	Q	R		2nd, Degree
10	11	12	13	14	15	16	17	18		
S	T	U	V	W	X	Y	Z			3rd, Degree
19	20	21	22	23	24	25	26			

A	B	C	D	E	F	G	H	I		1st, Degree
1	2	3	4	5	6	7	8	9		
J	K	L	M	N	O	P	Q	R		2nd, Degree
S	T	U	V	W	X	Y	Z			3rd, Degree
1	2	3	4	5	6	7	8			

NAMES   NUMBERS

_____   _____

_____   _____

_____   _____

THE GOAL may be contrary to the demands of the Expression but represents your inner feelings and understanding. It is found by adding the Month, Day, and Year of Birth.

A	B	C	D	E	F	G	H	I	1st. Degree
1	2	3	4	5	6	7	8	9	
J	K	L	M	N	O	P	Q	R	2nd. Degree
10	11	12	13	14	15	16	17	18	
S	T	U	V	W	X	Y	Z		3rd. Degree
19	20	21	22	23	24	25	26		

A	B	C	D	E	F	G	H	I	1st. Degree
1	2	3	4	5	6	7	8	9	
J	K	L	M	N	O	P	Q	R	2nd. Degree
S	T	U	V	W	X	Y	Z		3rd. Degree
1	2	3	4	5	6	7	8		

NAMES

NUMBERS

_____   _____

_____   _____

_____   _____

THE ACHIEVEMENT (9 Year Cycles) indicates the subconscious drives during each of the four Achievement cycles. First Achievement is found by adding the Birth Day to the Birth Month. Second Achievement is found by adding the Birth Day to the Birth Year. Third Achievement is found by adding the First and Second Achievement numbers together. Fourth Achievement is found by adding the Birth Year to the Birth Month. (See the Answer section for steps to determine the number of years in each cycle.)

A	B	C	D	E	F	G	H	I		1st, Degree
1	2	3	4	5	6	7	8	9		
J	K	L	M	N	O	P	Q	R		2nd, Degree
10	11	12	13	14	15	16	17	18		
S	T	U	V	W	X	Y	Z			3rd, Degree
19	20	21	22	23	24	25	26			

A	B	C	D	E	F	G	H	I		1st, Degree
1	2	3	4	5	6	7	8	9		
J	K	L	M	N	O	P	Q	R		2nd, Degree
S	T	U	V	W	X	Y	Z			3rd, Degree
1	2	3	4	5	6	7	8			

NAMES   NUMBERS

_____   _____

_____   _____

_____   _____

THE DEMANDS act as warning signals to the Achievements. A Demand is not a lacking quality but an ability which must be developed. First Demand is found by subtracting the Birth Month from the Birth Day. Second Demand is found by subtracting the Birth Day from the Birth Year. Third Demand is found by subtracting the smaller from the larger of the first two Demands. Fourth Demand is found by subtracting the Birth Year from the Birth Month. (See the Answer section for steps to determine the number of years in each cycle.)

A	B	C	D	E	F	G	H	I	1st, Degree
1	2	3	4	5	6	7	8	9	
J	K	L	M	N	O	P	Q	R	2nd, Degree
10	11	12	13	14	15	16	17	18	
S	T	U	V	W	X	Y	Z		3rd, Degree
19	20	21	22	23	24	25	26		

A	B	C	D	E	F	G	H	I	1st, Degree
1	2	3	4	5	6	7	8	9	
J	K	L	M	N	O	P	Q	R	2nd, Degree
S	T	U	V	W	X	Y	Z		3rd, Degree
1	2	3	4	5	6	7	8		

NAMES   NUMBERS

_____   _____

_____   _____

_____   _____

THE ALPHA-ATMOSPHERE is taken from the First Name only. Each letter of the First Name covers 9 years of the current time period. (See Answer section for procedures to set up the Time Chart.)

A	B	C	D	E	F	G	H	I	1st, Degree
1	2	3	4	5	6	7	8	9	
J	K	L	M	N	O	P	Q	R	2nd, Degree
10	11	12	13	14	15	16	17	18	
S	T	U	V	W	X	Y	Z		3rd, Degree
19	20	21	22	23	24	25	26		

A	B	C	D	E	F	G	H	I	1st, Degree
1	2	3	4	5	6	7	8	9	
J	K	L	M	N	O	P	Q	R	2nd, Degree
S	T	U	V	W	X	Y	Z		3rd, Degree
1	2	3	4	5	6	7	8		

NAMES   NUMBERS

_____   _____

_____   _____

_____   _____

THE ALPHA-PASSAGE shows you how to prepare for coming events, how to make changes, how to care for your health, when to marry, etc. It is based on the time cycle derived from each letter of the Full Name. (See Answer section for procedures to set up the Time Chart.)

A	B	C	D	E	F	G	H	I	1st, Degree
1	2	3	4	5	6	7	8	9	
J	K	L	M	N	O	P	Q	R	2nd, Degree
10	11	12	13	14	15	16	17	18	
S	T	U	V	W	X	Y	Z		3rd, Degree
19	20	21	22	23	24	25	26		

A	B	C	D	E	F	G	H	I	1st, Degree
1	2	3	4	5	6	7	8	9	
J	K	L	M	N	O	P	Q	R	2nd, Degree
S	T	U	V	W	X	Y	Z		3rd, Degree
1	2	3	4	5	6	7	8		

NAMES

_____

_____

_____

NUMBERS

_____

_____

_____

THE ESSENCE is the sum total of experience for the period in which it operates. It suggests what to do with the elements of your Time Chart. It is found by adding the letters from the Alpha-Atmosphere and the Alpha-Passage.

A	B	C	D	E	F	G	H	I		1st, Degree
1	2	3	4	5	6	7	8	9		
J	K	L	M	N	O	P	Q	R		2nd, Degree
10	11	12	13	14	15	16	17	18		
S	T	U	V	W	X	Y	Z			3rd, Degree
19	20	21	22	23	24	25	26			

A	B	C	D	E	F	G	H	I		1st, Degree
1	2	3	4	5	6	7	8	9		
J	K	L	M	N	O	P	Q	R		2nd, Degree
S	T	U	V	W	X	Y	Z			3rd, Degree
1	2	3	4	5	6	7	8			

NAMES   NUMBERS

_____   _____

_____   _____

_____   _____

THE ALPHA-AGE indicates potential conditions and changes during a particular year. It is found by adding the current age of the individual being charted to their age on the next birthday.

A	B	C	D	E	F	G	H	I	1st, Degree
1	2	3	4	5	6	7	8	9	
J	K	L	M	N	O	P	Q	R	2nd, Degree
10	11	12	13	14	15	16	17	18	
S	T	U	V	W	X	Y	Z		3rd, Degree
19	20	21	22	23	24	25	26		

A	B	C	D	E	F	G	H	I	1st, Degree
1	2	3	4	5	6	7	8	9	
J	K	L	M	N	O	P	Q	R	2nd, Degree
S	T	U	V	W	X	Y	Z		3rd, Degree
1	2	3	4	5	6	7	8		

NAMES   NUMBERS

_____   _____

_____   _____

_____   _____

THE PERSONAL YEAR sets the timeframe for the various conditions and changes discovered in the Time Chart. It is found by adding the Birth Month and Birth Day to the Universal Year.

A	B	C	D	E	F	G	H	I	1st, Degree
1	2	3	4	5	6	7	8	9	
J	K	L	M	N	O	P	Q	R	2nd, Degree
10	11	12	13	14	15	16	17	18	
S	T	U	V	W	X	Y	Z		3rd, Degree
19	20	21	22	23	24	25	26		

A	B	C	D	E	F	G	H	I	1st, Degree
1	2	3	4	5	6	7	8	9	
J	K	L	M	N	O	P	Q	R	2nd, Degree
S	T	U	V	W	X	Y	Z		3rd, Degree
1	2	3	4	5	6	7	8		

THE PERPETUAL CYCLE charts the seven fifty-two day cycles in the Personal Year, beginning with the Birth Day and continuing for 364 days. (See Answer section for directions.)

THE PERSONAL MONTH CYCLE is determined by adding the Birth Month to the Personal Year number.

NAMES   NUMBERS

_____   _____

_____   _____

_____   _____

THE OCCUPATIONAL GRAPH: See chart in Answer section.

NAMES   NUMBERS

_____   _____

_____   _____

_____   _____

THE YEAR COMPARISONS: See Answer section.

NAMES   NUMBERS

_____   _____

_____   _____

_____   _____

THE YEARLY ACHIEVEMENT is the addition of the Birth Month, the Birth Day, and the Personal Year numbers. First Achievement is found by adding the Birth Month and the Birth Day. Second Achievement is found by adding the Birth Day and the Personal Year numbers. Third Achievement is found by adding the First and Second Achievement numbers.

Fourth Achievement is found by adding the Personal Year and Birth Month numbers. See Answer section for details on 4 yearly cycles.

NAMES   NUMBERS

_____   _____

_____   _____

_____   _____

RULERSHIP OF THE BODY: See Answer section.

                                NUMBERS &
NAMES   RULERSHIPS

_____   _____

_____   _____

_____   _____

COLORS are intimately related to your personal numbers and can be used in conjunction with key elements of the Alphascan chart.

A. For Relaxation, wear the number of your Desire number
B. For Security, wear the color of your Resource number
C. To assert your Capabilities, wear the color of your Second Cycle Number
D. For Professional Advancement, wear the color of your Personal Year number

NAMES   NUMBER & COLOR

_____   _____

_____   _____

_____   _____